MOROCCAN TAGINE COOKBOOK FOR BEGINNERS

MOROCCAN TAGINE COOKBOOK
FOR BEGINNERS

75 One-Pot Recipes

KARIMA ELATCHI

Photography by DARREN MUIR

R

ROCKRIDGE PRESS

First Rockridge Press trade paperback edition 2022

Rockridge Press and the Rockridge Press logo are trademarks or registered trademarks of Callisto Media Inc. and/or its affiliates in the United States and other countries and may not be used without written permission.

For general information on our other products and services, please contact our Customer Care Department within the United States at (866) 744-2665, or outside the United States at (510) 253-0500.

Paperback ISBN: 978-1-63878-867-6
eBook ISBN: 978-1-63878-515-6

Manufactured in the United States of America

Interior and Cover Designer: Angela Navarra
Art Producer: Hannah Dickerson
Editor: Anne Goldberg and Leah Zarra
Production Editor: Rachel Taenzler
Production Manager: Martin Worthington

Photography © 2022 Darren Muir, food styling by Yolanda Muir
Cover image: Roasted Chicken with Green Apples and Green Olives (page 70)

10 9 8 7 6 5 4 3 2 1 0

In the memory
of my loving parents,
who helped me become
who I am today.
I dedicate this
cookbook
to them.

CONTENTS

INTRODUCTION

As with all ancient cultures, Moroccan food reflects the diversity of the past and the shared ingredients from its neighboring countries making its cuisine a unique global experience. To celebrate the culinary wealth of my ancestors, I take great pride in the creation of authentic, organic, and savory dishes. You too can create these same timeless, earthy tagine dishes with patience and practice. The tagine falls into the "one-pot dish" category and is layered with complexities to savor. It is the perfect dish for an amateur cook to stretch their imagination and wow their family and friends!

My recipes originate from my heritage and from people who shared their knowledge with me. I grew up in Morocco, where my dear parents, Mohamed and Zahrah, instilled and fostered the love of learning in me from my early years. My mother prepared every meal from scratch with fresh olives, wheat, barley, olive oil, honey, and aromatic herbs, all delivered from the yearly harvest of her father's land. She prepped and designed myriad stackable foods for the pantry. So, as the oldest girl, my passion for cooking started at an early age as I watched my mom cooking, creating dishes, and always setting an appetizing meal on the dinner table. I grew up knowing details about spices and cooking methods. On the other hand, my father encouraged me to pursue an academic life, which led me to graduate from the Institute of Programming in 1985, and I was hired by the minister of finance, where I worked for fifteen years. I never imagined cooking would become the center of my life as I spent years in an office–even after getting married created a new space for me in my own kitchen where I celebrated all my culinary skills.

My next journey continued in the United States, where the diversity of the international community inspired me and cooking was a strong link to my roots. Being alone here in a new country, I cooked and shared with my neighbors, and created connections to so many people. One day I invited all the neighbors in my building to an outdoor party, and people enjoyed my food so much they asked me to teach them. I immediately started teaching cooking classes one day a week, which grew to twice a week as the group got bigger.

The trust these people placed in me encouraged me to license my kitchen and start selling cookies and appetizers, then preparing orders for events, and even catering a full wedding. All this success gave me the confidence to do more. So, when I moved to a bigger city, my catering and teaching journey expanded, and I was hired to teach cooking classes at a local college.

As my confidence grew, I opened my first restaurant in Corvallis, Oregon, to celebrate Moroccan food. The space invited everyone to experience the taste of exotic food while partaking in a Moroccan experience. In less than a year, my business earned the honor of the best restaurant in the area! And when time permitted, I catered for important organizations and events until I eventually moved back to online orders and teaching classes. I noticed that simplified cooking drew people, which led me to improvise with one-pot recipes featuring the tagine. This one-pot dish both communicates all the earthy flavors as well as being perfect for people who want to experiment with an exotic cuisine in a simplified, easy-to-cook way.

Although my career began in programming, food always pulled at my apron strings, and I hope you allow yourself the gift of cooking one clay pot at a time. My dear friends, I provide you with a straightforward passage to successful tagine cooking. Remember, if you love Moroccan food but believe you may not have the necessary skills, my 75 recipes will allow you to delve step-by-step into this easy-to-read book that will lead you to enjoyable, successful cooking!

CHAPTER 1

TAGINE 101

So, you might be standing in your kitchen contemplating the brand new conical-shaped cooking vessel sitting on your counter, perhaps wondering what to do with this new acquisition. Or maybe you intend to get a tagine and need guidance on choosing the perfect one. No matter your situation, this chapter covers all that you need to know about the Moroccan tagine. By the end, the tagine will no longer be mysterious; you will understand its history and importance to Moroccan cuisine, the benefits of using this special pot, and how it produces such delectable food. Don't own a tagine yet? No problem! I will outline what vessel to use instead (before your tagine arrives) and what features to look for when purchasing a tagine—plus how to maintain, clean, and even repair chips.

WHAT IS A TAGINE?

The word "tagine" or "tajine" refers to both the traditional clay or earthenware pot used for cooking and serving as well as to the slow-cooked dish that is cooked in this vessel. The word is derived from both Amazigh Arabic (ṭagin) "shallow earthen pot" and from Ancient Greek (tágēnon) meaning "frying pan." The first written mention of tagine is found in a well-known ninth-century Arabic story collection called *One Thousand and One Nights*. These vessels were crucial portable ovens used by North African nomads for preparing food on the move.

The tagine was used throughout Moroccan history as a multipurpose tool for all cooking. It features a wide, flat, low-sided circular base and a top molded into a cone-shaped dome that tapers to a knob on top that serves as the handle. Putting the two pieces together creates an incredibly effective oven of sorts.

The traditional tagine was made of clay with no glaze or paint, and the construction of these pots creates a unique cooking environment. What makes the tagine different from another cooking vessel is the way the lid is shaped and how that impacts the food that is cooked in the pot. As the food cooks, steam from the liquid and ingredients rises into the cone-shaped lid, condenses, and falls back into the dish. This means the dish is naturally and continuously basted, so the ingredients stay moist and the meat tenderizes. It's not necessary to use a lot of liquid when cooking in a tagine because it doesn't evaporate but recycles again and again until the flavors are rich and condensed. You might be thinking this sounds like slow cooking or the results of cooking in a Dutch oven, but these vessels do not produce the taste-of-the-earth flavor attributed to an unglazed clay tagine.

A tagine is traditionally cooked over charcoal or wood, with enough space between the heat source and pot so the temperature stays low and steady. Charcoal is used specifically for its ability to keep perfect heat for hours. If you want, you can cook a tagine over charcoal, but an electric or gas stovetop works beautifully when the tagine is placed on a diffuser and the heat is kept low.

A tagine—the dish that is cooked in the pot of the same name—is a rich mixture of meat, poultry, or fish, and includes vegetables or fruits, aromatic spices, dried fruits, and nuts. Tagines can also be vegetables alone, which still make a delicious meal.

BENEFITS OF USING A TAGINE

The tagine is at the heart of my cooking because of its link to tradition and its endless benefits. The tagine may seem like a limited tool, but its uses are myriad, much like a cast-iron pan or Dutch oven. Tagines are durable and beautiful and can easily be transferred directly to the table to double as a serving dish. Here are just a few other benefits to consider:

DELICIOUS, EASY RESULTS

The distinctive shape of the tagine is not just aesthetically pleasing, but also it has a functional basis. As the dish cooks, steam is trapped by the conical lid and runs back down its sides into the food below, concentrating the flavors. This method of cooking can turn any dish into a delicious meal, and a beginner cook can layer in simple ingredients and pop the lid on for a variety of one-pot dishes.

BETTER THAN SLOW-COOKED

Unlike its closest kitchen tool cousin, the slow cooker, the tagine produces a delightful, caramelized finish as liquid cooks off and is reabsorbed by the ingredients. Also, there is an indefinable, dare I say magical, earthy taste of clay in the food cooked in it if you use an unglazed vessel.

STOVE TO TABLE

Tagine recipes are not only one-pot cooking, but they also combine cooking and serving into a single dish, which minimizes the cleaning after the meal is complete. Believe me, there's a bit of excitement when an earthy and ethnically designed tagine is set on the table—not to mention the mystery of what's under the lid. Once the cone is removed and the incredible smell and beautiful textured dish is revealed, you might find yourself sensing its history and sharing in the charm of the Old World.

TAGINE COOKING IS VERSATILE

The tagine is traditionally set into embers or on charcoal braziers, but you can use yours on the stovetop with a heat diffuser on very low heat. Many tagines can also be placed in the oven, although this defeats the purpose of its conical design (even though the tagine will still be tasty). In higher heat environments like an oven, or when the lid is left off, the steam is not condensed back into the other ingredients.

A tagine is famous for cooking savory stews, but this vessel is associated with all kinds of Moroccan cooking. The tagine can cook a variety of dishes, from breakfasts to side dishes to desserts. Although the tagine is designed for low and slow cooking, the enclosed environment works for recipes with shorter cook times as well. There are recipes that are cooked in the tagine base (sans lid) in the oven similar to a cast-iron skillet or baking dish. Some recipes that can be adapted to a tagine include:

◊ **Breakfast:** Frittata, omelets (see Tagine Omelet, page 164), quiche, and shakshuka (see Roasted Bell Pepper, Tomato, and Roasted Garlic Shakshuka, page 152).

◊ **Sides:** Sautéed or braised vegetables, "roasted" root vegetables (potatoes, sweet potatoes, carrots, beets, parsnips), or squash (butternut, pumpkin, acorn).

◊ **Main courses:** Whole Roasted Stuffed Chicken (page 92), Beef Meatballs in Spicy Tomato Sauce with Eggs (page 48), or Spicy Baked Fish in Harissa Tomato Sauce with Olives (page 110).

◊ **Sweet:** Though often used in savory stews, baked or braised fruit, such as apples, pears, peaches, and apricots, can also be cooked to serve on their own.

TAGINE AND MOROCCAN FOOD

The tagine pot is an invention often attributed to the Berbers—who call themselves Amazigh—who were the pre-Arab nomadic inhabitants of North Africa. Tagine is the only vessel that has been used for cooking throughout the entire history of Moroccan cuisine. In some regions of the country, it is still the *only* cookware used. Tagines—the dishes, not the pot—date from the very origins of Moroccan cuisine. These beloved recipes are at the heart of traditional meals and are named after the earthenware pot in which they are cooked. Wonderful eclectic meals suit the tagine, including breakfast omelets, various meats such as lamb, beef, and poultry, fish, both main and side vegetarian dishes, legumes, and even bread.

Different tagines represent a variety of incredible, delicious tastes and textures based on native spices and herbs from the various regions of Morocco. Northern Morocco and most coastal cities specialize in seafood tagines using chermoula–a marinade of garlic, cilantro, parsley, lemon, olive oil, cumin, and harissa. Western Morocco, an agricultural region, features tagines of lamb, beef, poultry, wild birds, rabbits, and seasonal vegetables. Southern Morocco, known for its hot, desert-like climate, offers camel meat, goat, and lamb tagines. Eastern Morocco specializes in cow's feet, tripe, chicken, and beef tagines. One of the common threads that runs through these rich, gloriously flavorful recipes is the distinctive cooking vessel used to make them. So, how do you choose a tagine to cook the delicious recipes in this book? Let's find out!

CHOOSING A TAGINE

Though the tagine is a simple cooking vessel, it comes in many types; it can be challenging to choose one. They used to be difficult to find outside of Morocco for a reasonable price, but now companies mass-produce them, so tagines are affordable and accessible. They have become popular due to online sources such as eBay, Amazon, and other sites that sell them worldwide. You can also find tagines locally at international markets or kitchen supply stores. Make sure you pick one meant for cooking and not just serving because many stores sell handcrafted, decorative tagines that look lovely but are unsuitable for using over a heat source. The best tagine for cooking will look like natural raw clay, plain or minimally decorated. Most serving vessels will be clearly marked as unsuitable for heating, but a good rule is tagines meant for cooking are simpler, heavier, and unadorned. It is best to ask a store associate to be safe that your tagine is meant for cooking. Some features to consider when purchasing your tagine are what material it is made of, size, weight, design, and cost.

Traditional tagines are made of clay or earthenware, both materials are common in Morocco, and they can be unglazed or glazed. Unglazed earthenware or clay will produce an authentic tagine taste and cooking experience, but this vessel requires more care and should come from a reputable manufacturer. You can also find tagines that are lead-free glazed "flameware" (flameproof ceramic cookware), enameled cast iron, or metal (aluminum or stainless steel). Each type of material has pros and cons to consider, so when purchasing a tagine, research which one best suits your lifestyle, recipes, and budget. My recommendation would be to choose one that is simple and unglazed, not shiny, with an earthy look and texture. It should be a little heavy, with a tightly fitting lid, and no trace of cracks inside the lid or the bottom of the base. Also, choose the right size for your needs.

Tagines come in many sizes. Small ones with no cover are used for cooking omelets or sautéing vegetables for breakfast. They are very light and easy to use, and since they are usually less than $40, you can have several at home for cooking side dishes.

Larger tagines are for cooking entrées—including deep tagines used for soups, stews, broths, or to steam couscous. Large unglazed or cast-iron tagines can be quite heavy, especially when the lid is on, so keep in mind having to heft the pot when cooking and cleaning to help you decide on the size and material. The price of a tagine varies depending on where it is made or sold, its size, and material—with cast iron and flameware the most expensive because of their durability. These materials will not impart the distinctive clay flavor to your food, but they are versatile and can be used on the stovetop and in the oven.

Whatever tagine you choose, a well-made tagine is worth the price, because a genuine Moroccan vessel can produce healthy and authentic meals for years.

ACCESSORIES

The tagine is a one-pot cooking method, but depending on your tagine, it might need some accessories to ensure success. Some accessories that are important (or traditional) include:

Berrad: A *berrad* is a silver teapot that can come with decorative tea glasses and a silver tray for serving a traditional tagine meal.

Gsaa: A big clay tray, a *gsaa* is used for mixing bread dough or tossing couscous.

Heat diffuser: If using a gas or electric stove—and a clay or earthenware tagine—a heat diffuser is necessary to protect the tagine from direct contact with the heating element. A heat diffuser is a flat metal disc that acts as a protective layer between direct heat from the stove burner and the tagine. It also ensures the heat is spread out rather than concentrated on one spot. Heat diffusers can be either solid metal or have perforations that allow air to flow through, which helps dissipate the heat. Either choice will work when cooking on an electric or gas stove.

Majmar: A *majmar* is a charcoal brazier used as a heat source. Traditionally, tagines are cooked directly on wood embers (*kanoon*), but a *majmar* is more convenient.

Tbiqa: A woven basket with a lid, the *tbiqa* is used as a bread box.

Wooden spoon: A big wooden spoon for serving or used between the base of the tagine and the lid for venting.

TAGINE ALTERNATIVES

The beauty of the tagine is it is a slow cooker and serving dish all in one. The magic of tagine cooking comes from its cone-shaped lid, but you still can create gorgeous tagine meals if you don't own a tagine pot.

Alternatives to the tagine can be any heavy, wide, shallow dish or skillet with a tight-fitting lid. A Dutch oven is probably the closest to the tagine because its cast-iron construction provides even heat at low or high. You can also try an Instant Pot or slow cooker for a similar result to a tagine. These appliances require no supervision, so are convenient, but you might miss the lovely caramelization and wonderful earthy flavor imparted by a traditional clay or earthenware tagine.

USING YOUR TAGINE

So, you have a new tagine sitting on your counter and you are ready to create some delicious food. Do you need to do anything first or can you just jump into the recipes? The tagine cooking method is not complicated, but following some basic steps can get you familiar with the technique and help you build confidence. These instructions are for cooking a basic tagine; some recipes might require the addition of ingredients later in the cooking time, such as fruit, olives, tender vegetables, or legumes. Let's walk through using your tagine!

1. **Season your tagine.** If this is your first time cooking with a clay or earthenware tagine, it must first be seasoned to prevent food from sticking and the dish from fissuring. For an unglazed tagine, this will also remove the taste of raw clay. Submerge the tagine base and lid entirely in water overnight, remove it, and dry it completely (under the sun if possible). After a few hours, brush the interior and exterior of the lid and base generously with olive oil and place them in a cold oven. Heat the oven to 300° F and bake the tagine for 3 hours to seal the surface pores of the clay and create a natural glaze. Turn off the oven, let the tagine completely cool, and rub it dry with a towel. If you purchased an enameled flameware or metal tagine, you might be able to just wash it and start cooking. If it's uncoated cast iron, it will have its own seasoning method. Check the manufacturer's instructions to see if this step is required.

2. **Marinate the protein.** If the recipe has a marinated protein, then you will do this first. Mix up the marinade in a bowl, add the protein, and marinate for at least 15 minutes and up to 1 hour or overnight in the refrigerator. The longer you marinate, the more intense the flavor.

3. **Arrange the base layer.** First, the tagine is rubbed with some oil. After that, my mom used to lay parsley or cilantro sprigs and celery across the base of the tagine as the first layer, but many recipes use a layer of thickly sliced or chopped onions to keep the meat from sticking to the bottom and burning during cooking.

4. **Layer tomatoes or other vegetables.** This step is not in all recipes, but you will often add a layer of tomato sauce or tomatoes and other vegetables such as carrots on top of the onions.

5. **Add the meat, poultry, or seafood.** Place the protein either on the base layer or work from the center out, leaving a border free around the edges if adding more vegetables or garlic. You might also pile more vegetables or other ingredients such as legumes or fruit on top of the protein.

6. **Add the liquid, oil, and spices.** Liquid, such as water, and oil are added. Sometimes the water is used to rinse out the flavorful ingredients from the bowl that held the marinade or spice paste. The liquid is then poured around the sides of the tagine so it doesn't wash the flavorful spices off the ingredients.

7. **Place the tagine on the heat source.** Cover the tagine and place it on a heat diffuser on a stove burner set to very low heat.

8. **Cook in the tagine.** Bring the tagine to a very slow simmer and cook according to the recipe instructions. The time will vary depending on the ingredients, between 40 minutes to 1 hour for eggs, vegetarian dishes, and fish, and 2 to 3 hours for poultry, beef, and lamb.

9. **Check the liquid level and add secondary ingredients.** Check your liquid at the intervals recommended in the recipe and adjust as needed. You do not want to thin the sauce too much but need to prevent the tagine from cooking dry. You are looking for about ½ inch of liquid at the bottom.

10. **Garnish.** Remove the tagine from the heat and let it cool for 5 to 10 minutes. Then garnish it with herbs, olives, sesame seeds, scallions, preserved lemon, or other ingredients.

CLEANING AND MAINTENANCE

The care of your tagine depends on its material, so make sure you read the enclosed instructions from the manufacturer. My preference is an unglazed clay tagine, even though this vessel is very delicate and requires specific cleaning and maintenance to keep it in good condition. Do not wash your unglazed tagine with soap or soak it in any liquid because the porous clay will absorb it, which will impart an unpleasant flavor to your food. Never use coarse metal sponges because this would remove the patina. When washing an unglazed tagine after use, it is best to pour in warm water when it is empty and use salt and a wooden spoon to scrub the residue and grease. Then apply a mixture of baking soda and vinegar, rinse well with warm water, and dry the tagine with a clean towel. When your tagine is thoroughly dry, lightly coat the interior of the lid and the base with olive oil before storing it uncovered to promote air circulation and prevent mold. If the tagine happens to develop mold, don't worry; just wash it as usual, dry it, bake it, season it with olive oil, and, voilà, it is like new and ready for your cooking journey.

I always recommend an unglazed clay tagine, because the glaze on the tagine prevents all those delicious flavors from permeating the clay. If you have a glazed tagine, it can be washed like other cookware because the coating protects it from absorbing anything. In most cases, glazed tagines can be washed in the dishwasher, but double-check with the manufacturer's instructions. The best way to maintain a tagine is to use it regularly.

SERVING FOOD

The tagine is always a centerpiece of any Moroccan dining table. Although in the United States people associate tagines with couscous, in Morocco tagines are always served with fresh homemade bread. In addition, spicy olives, harissa, vegetable salad, and naturally carbonated water are a must for any meal. Traditionally, in Morocco, the tagine is shared with family members or friends, all sitting around the table, using their hands and the fresh bread to dip into the tagine pot, scooping out the tender meat, vegetables, and sauce, enjoying the meal as they relax and talk. After finishing the delectable food, Moroccan green mint tea with seasonal herbs is served on a silver tray with tea glasses and teapot, with Moroccan biscotti. The meal is a precious time to commune with loved ones and partake in an exquisitely prepared tagine.

• WHAT IF IT'S CHIPPED? •

Traditional tagines made of unglazed clay are very delicate. Despite this, a tagine is designed to last a long time, and as it gets older, it gets stronger. Cracks are undesirable but perfectly normal, and unless you have an extra tagine, knowing how to fix cracks is crucial.

Most deeper cracks, often the result of exposing the tagine to extreme heat differences or too little liquid, are difficult to fix at home. But you can fix smaller cracks or leaks by mixing 2 teaspoons of water with 1 teaspoon of all-purpose flour to create a thick paste. Spread the paste on both sides of the crack and all around it and set it over very low heat to dry the paste completely. Leave the paste on the tagine until the vessel is completely cool after cooking and repeat the process if necessary.

ESSENTIAL TAGINE SKILLS

Cooking traditions and complex flavors are profoundly important to Moroccan cooking culture. For centuries, the tagine was essential to the way these aromatic meals were prepared. Tagine cooking does not require the skills of a master chef, but a few techniques will make it easier for you to create delicious tagine meals.

KNIFE SKILLS

Cooking with a tagine is all about how the ingredients are layered on top of one another, and this requires cutting the meat, poultry, fish, and veggies a specific way. Meat needs to be cut in 3- to 4-inch pieces, with poultry and fish cut in quarters, halves, or whole. For onions used as the bottom layer to provide protection from the heat, the slices need to be about ⅓ inch thick; any thinner and they will burn. Other veggies layered around and on the top of the meat should be bigger pieces, so they hold their shape in the low and slow cooking process.

LAYERING

The first step of tagine cooking is to layer vegetables across the base of the tagine pot, creating a cushion for the remaining ingredients. This method will keep the meat from sticking to the bottom and burning during cooking. I often use a layer of parsley, cilantro, and celery stems—just like my mom taught me—on the bottom, then onions, then the meat in the middle, leaving enough room to arrange the vegetables around the meat and less on the top. Keep in mind you will not be stirring the recipe, so whatever arrangement you create will be the final presentation when you serve.

SEASONING

Seasoning is essential in a tagine because there is no stirring while the recipe cooks. So, over many years I have developed an easy method of seasoning tagines that's ideal for beginners! In a small bowl, mix all the spices required for your dish, including salt and garlic, then add a little water and mix until you get a thick paste. Rub some of this paste on any meat, poultry, or fish in the recipe before you layer it in the tagine. Add a bit of olive oil and water to the remaining spice paste in the bowl and pour it evenly over all the layers in your tagine.

GARNISHING

My mom always said that your eyes eat before your mouth. So, the final presentation of the dish is an essential part of tagine cooking. Garnishing your tagine makes all your work look appetizing and boosts the cuisine to another level. Some garnishes like olives, preserved lemon, or dried fruit should be added about 15 minutes before the recipe is complete, so they are juicy and hold their shape. Other garnishes are added after the cooking is complete and the tagine is still hot, like chopped herbs or nuts, so they stay fresh looking or keep their crunch.

ADDING WATER

The tagine is designed to require only a small amount of water for cooking, because for the nomads living in the desert, water was scarce. Cooking with a tagine is all about the richness of the constantly condensing liquid. Most recipes start with 1 cup of liquid for small tagines and 2½ cups for larger ones, and you need to monitor the amount to ensure it doesn't dry out. The level of liquid will fluctuate as it condenses back into the dish and will depend on the type of meat or veggies used, because some vegetables absorb more liquid whereas others release it during the cooking.

Take extra care to check the liquid and add boiling water (pouring around the edge of the ingredients) as needed. Remember, in most recipes, you want a sauce reduced to the consistency of a medium gravy—not too thin or thick. Always add water by sight, even if a recipe indicates to add more, as not all ingredients absorb water the same way. Extra tip: Pour the water in the lid's knob to create extra steam for the dish.

COOKING

Tagine cooking is famous for its slow-cooked method. Traditionally, this vessel is placed over wood embers or on a charcoal brazier. The other more common option outside of Morocco is on the stovetop, using a heat diffuser, over low to medium-low heat until it reaches a slow simmer. Some tagines can be placed in the oven, which can be the preferred method for big pieces of lamb shoulder or leg, whole chicken, or a big, whole fish. Check the manufacturer's manual to see if oven cooking is advised for your tagine. The cooking time will vary depending on the base ingredients in a recipe and the size of the meat, poultry, or fish, if using; poultry, fish, and veggies take less time and beef or lamb take longer. Abrupt changes in temperature can cause the tagine to crack—always bring the tagine to room temperature (for example, if removing it from the refrigerator) before placing it on a hot surface; and when the tagine is done cooking, never place it directly on a cold surface.

THE FLAVORS OF MOROCCO

Over the centuries, Moroccan cuisine has been influenced by interactions and trade with other cultures and nations, including Arabs from the Arabian Peninsula; Moorish refugees from Andalusia; Portuguese invaders; and Roman, French, and Spanish colonialists. Each of these civilizations contributed to the unique character of modern Moroccan food. Moroccan cuisine has a sweet and savory flavor profile. Arabs are the ones who brought the famous spices from China, India, and Malaysia, such as cinnamon, ginger, paprika, cumin, and turmeric. However, most spices used in the cuisine are indigenous to Morocco.

This diverse and rich history might seem intimidating and the food difficult to create. Don't worry, this wonderful culinary journey isn't complicated. I feel cooking must be a joy, especially when you are new to a cuisine. So, I have created easy tagine recipes with simple instructions, and I will guide you through the spices, aromatics, and pantry items needed to create flavorful, spectacular dishes that are sure to delight you.

SPICES AND HERBS

A wide variety of spices are used in Moroccan cuisine to create a rich and flavorful meal. It is not about the quantity of spices in a recipe; it is about freshness and quality. Moroccan recipes are not overpoweringly spicy, but rather the *fragrance* of each spice infuses the food. These wonderful spices are more accessible in countries outside of Morocco because people are open to changing their cooking to include global influences. You can buy any of these spices in local stores in many countries and online on Etsy, World Market, Amazon, and Moroccan websites. I suggest you avoid blends until you are familiar with the taste of the individual spices. There are daily, basic spices in Moroccan cuisine—black pepper, turmeric, cinnamon, cumin, ginger, and paprika—and spices for special days, like saffron, cardamom, mace, nutmeg, and anise seed. As you become familiar with each spice, you will discover personal favorites that appeal to your palate.

◊ **Anise seed:** Sweet, aromatic licorice flavor

◊ **Bay leaf:** Almost minty flavor

◊ **Black pepper:** Pungent smell and hot taste

◊ **Caraway:** Nutty, bittersweet, and sharp with a hint of citrus and anise

◊ **Cardamom:** Strong, fruity, sweet, pungent flavor and aroma

◊ **Cilantro:** Tangy citrus flavor with leaves similar to parsley

◊ **Cinnamon:** Aromatic, sweet, and woody flavor

◊ **Cloves:** Intense and aromatic, with sweet, warm undertones

◊ **Coriander seed:** Dried seeds of the coriander plant with a spicy, citrus flavor

◊ **Cumin seed:** Rich and earthy, warm with an edge of citrus

◊ **Fennel seed:** Similar to anise in flavor but less intense, with a warm and sweet aroma

◊ **Fenugreek:** Sweet, nutty flavor, incredibly bitter seeds used in curry powder—famous in Morocco for a dish called *rfissa*

◊ **Ginger:** Dried, ground ginger root, spicy, warm, sweetish, and sharp

◊ **Lemon verbena:** Used dried or fresh in teas

◊ **Mace:** The outer covering of the nutmeg seed; slightly warm and sweet taste

◊ **Nutmeg:** Delicately warm, spicy, and sweet; best if freshly grated

◊ **Oregano:** Sweet and spicy, bold and earthy with a hint of bitterness

◊ **Paprika:** Ranges from mild and sweet to very hot, with a bright color and a fruity, slightly bitter flavor

◊ **Parsley:** Clean and peppery taste with a touch of earthiness

◊ **Saffron:** Golden color, pungent, earthy, and grassy flavor and aroma, yet sweet; the most expensive spice in the world

◊ **Sesame seed:** Oil-rich seeds; mild, sweet, and nutty flavor and crunchy

◊ **Turmeric:** Earthy, peppery flavor and bright color

• STARRING SPICES: RAS EL HANOUT •

Morocco's most famous spice blend is called ras el hanout. This staple is a combination of high-quality spices, and its name means "top of the shop." You can of course purchase this blend, but one way to ensure your spices are the best is to grind them yourself and gently toast them in a dry skillet over low heat—taking care not to burn them. Ras el hanout has no definite recipe, but my favorite is:

2 teaspoons ground cardamom

2 teaspoons ground ginger

2 teaspoons ground mace

1 teaspoon ground cinnamon

1 teaspoon ground coriander

1 teaspoon freshly grated nutmeg

1 teaspoon ground turmeric

½ teaspoon ground allspice

½ teaspoon freshly ground black pepper

½ teaspoon ground cumin

½ teaspoon fennel seeds

½ teaspoon ground white pepper

¼ teaspoon ground cloves

In a small bowl, combine all the spices (toasted if desired) until well mixed. Transfer the spice blend to an airtight container and store in a cool, dry place for up to 1 month.

AROMATICS

In Western cuisine, aromatics are considered to be onions, celery, and garlic, which make up the base of many recipes. But this ingredient list goes further when it comes to Moroccan cuisine, and especially tagine cooking. Aromatics refers to spices, herbs, vegetables, meat, poultry, and fish—all of which contribute to the incredible flavors and aroma of the dishes.

All meat tagines start with a layer of onions; sometimes celery stalks or herb stems are added for extra flavor. So, every ingredient in the tagine plays a role, including onions, garlic, all meats, bone marrow, poultry, seafood, herbs, spices, preserved lemon, saffron, vegetables, and fruits. All tagines have different flavors and aromas, from sweet to savory to spicy, and when all are combined result in a well-rounded dish.

CONDIMENTS AND PANTRY

Moroccan dishes require very little in the way of special ingredients. They rely heavily on pantry staples and fresh produce as the base. That said, the Moroccan pantry probably varies a bit from the items you might typically have on hand, but a well-stocked pantry with a variety of essential Moroccan ingredients can ensure your time spent in the kitchen is enjoyable, easy, and efficient. Some of the pantry items can be homemade if you have time (see the staple recipes in chapter 6, page 167), but store-bought can work just as well. This list will give you an idea of what to have on hand if you plan to cook tagine recipes regularly.

◊ Almonds, blanched

◊ Butter and smen (Moroccan preserved and aged butter)

◊ Couscous, instant or regular

◊ Dates

◊ Dried fruit (raisins, apricots, prunes, cranberries, figs)

◊ Flour (all-purpose, whole-wheat, semolina, barley)

◊ Harissa, store-bought or homemade (page 174)

◊ Honey

◊ Legumes (chickpeas, lentils, split peas, fava beans, white beans), dried or canned

◊ Olive oil, extra-virgin

◊ Olives (black, green, or purple)

◊ Orange blossom water

- ◊ Pearl onions, pickled
- ◊ Pine nuts
- ◊ Preserved lemon, store-bought or homemade (page 172)
- ◊ Rice (basmati, jasmine, brown)
- ◊ Roasted eggplant paste
- ◊ Roasted peppers, store-bought
- ◊ Sheeba (a type of wormwood), for tea
- ◊ Tea (green, gunpowder, mint)
- ◊ Vinegar
- ◊ Yeast

• GETTING THE GOODS •

Mediterranean, North African, and Indian markets are the best place to shop for Moroccan ingredients. Look for the one near you, take a trip, and stock your pantry with a variety of staples like preserved lemon, harissa, olives, and more. Some stores have fresh meat, poultry, and produce as well. These markets are usually an exciting treasure trove of spices—so, read the ingredients, smell them (if possible), and pick whatever suits you.

Regular grocery stores will carry many items in the organic and international aisles. Look in stores like Whole Foods, New Seasons Market, or Trader Joe's for fresh and organic substitutes, staples, or other items like chickpeas, dried fruits, harissa, and even preserved lemon.

If you don't have international markets in your area, many staples and specialty items are available online.

TOOLS AND EQUIPMENT

Besides a stocked pantry, what makes your cooking journey an easy one is having the right tools—this will simplify all the preparations for your cooking. It is an excellent idea to have an extra tagine and diffuser for emergencies.

MUST-HAVE

◇ **Box grater:** Box graters should be sturdy (with nonslip handles) and have different sizes of holes for different preparation including grating, shredding, zesting, and slicing.

◇ **Cooling rack:** Use this for setting the tagine on to cool after cooking.

◇ **Diffuser:** If using the stovetop and your tagine is clay or earthenware, you'll need a diffuser to set over your stove burner.

◇ **Garlic press:** Garlic is a common ingredient in Moroccan cooking, so a garlic press will save lots of time chopping and mincing.

◇ **Instant-read thermometer:** Use this to check that your proteins are cooked through.

◇ **Knives:** Nothing beats a good-quality, sharp knife for cooking. Get a selection of knives, including a chef's knife, paring knife, and a utility knife.

◇ **Ladle:** This is good for serving from the tagine.

◇ **Measuring cups and spoons:** These are essential for accurate recipe reproduction. Pick up a set of dry measuring cups, a liquid measuring cup, and a set of measuring spoons.

◇ **Mixing bowls:** An assortment of bowls makes preparation and marinating simple. Stainless steel bowls are easy to clean and heatproof, but use glass or whatever material suits you.

◇ **Oven mitts:** These are necessary for transferring hot tagines from the stovetop or oven to a cooling rack.

◇ **Sieve:** A large sieve is essential for draining and rinsing canned beans.

◇ **Skimmer:** Use this to transfer pieces of meat or poultry from sauces to serve over couscous or rice. The sauce can then be ladled over separately.

◇ **Tagines:** It's ideal to have more than one tagine, in different sizes; most of the recipes in this book will be cooked in a lidded tagine.

◇ **Vegetable peeler:** Vegetables are the base of most tagines, so you will be doing lots of peeling. Pick up a peeler that is comfortable in your hand and sharp.

◇ **Wooden spoons:** These are great for stirring without damaging the surface of a tagine.

NICE TO HAVE

◇ **Electric kettle:** Use this to have hot water at the ready for you to adjust the water in a tagine as it cooks.

◇ **Food processor or blender:** The appliance you choose depends on your needs. A food processor is more expensive and can do everything a blender can as well as slice, grate, and puree large quantities of produce.

◇ **Mandoline:** This versatile slicer prepares veggies quickly and evenly in various cuts such as sliced, diced, and batons.

◇ **Mortar and pestle:** Called a *mehraz*, this is the best way to grind all kind of spices. It is also used for making chermoula and other herb mixtures.

◇ **Spice grinder:** For freshly ground spices, just a quick blitz and you are ready to cook. A coffee grinder works for this task as well.

◇ **Unlidded tagine:** For some recipes, you may want a small, unlidded tagine for sautéing vegetables or cooking eggs.

◇ **Zester:** Grating citrus zest is possible on a box grater, but a small, dedicated tool is handy.

SUBSTITUTIONS

The recipes in this book use ingredients found in most grocery stores—either in the regular aisles or the organic or international sections—but sometimes products are unavailable, or you don't have them handy when you want to cook a specific dish. Here are some easy substitutions for common Moroccan ingredients that will produce similar flavor results:

INGREDIENT	SUBSTITUTE
Harissa	Sambal oelek, sriracha
Preserved lemon	Lemon juice and grated zest
Ras el hanout	Garam masala (use half the amount called for), seven spices, baharat
Smen	Ghee, clarified butter
Saffron	Turmeric
Ground coriander	Ground cumin, ground caraway, garam masala
Date or pomegranate molasses	Regular molasses
Orange blossom water	Orange oil, orange zest

• A TOAST TO THE TAGINE •

Mint tea holds a very important place in Moroccan culture. It is traditionally drunk at any time of the day, but especially with or at the end of the meal, like a digestive. The tea is made of green tea or strong Chinese tea (gunpowder), hot water, sugar, and fresh or dried herbs. It is served in a uniquely shaped silver teapot called a *berrad*, along with beautiful colored and patterned tea glasses arranged on an engraved silver tray.

Moroccan tea is flavored with mint, marjoram, sage, oregano, orange blossom flower, and a type of wormwood known as *sheeba* (which is seasonal in the winter). Big celebrations or holidays feature tea mostly flavored with spearmint and orange blossom water. Since herbs are seasonal, people in Morocco dry them and combine them in a fragrant mixture, which gives the tea an amazing aroma and unique flavor.

Another popular beverage is Moroccan spiced coffee, though it's not an everyday drink like mint tea. The spiced coffee is made of freshly ground coffee, nutmeg, cloves, cinnamon, anise seed, ginger, star anise, cardamom, and black pepper. This combination of spices with coffee marries beautifully and creates a delicious fragrance that is the best way to wrap up a generous meal.

Seafood or vegetarian tagines are often accompanied by delicious vegetable, herb, and spice smoothies. Some common combinations include:

◊ Avocado, spinach, and lemon juice

◊ Beets and lemon juice

◊ Carrots, orange juice, and cinnamon

◊ Cucumber, lemon, and oregano

◊ Lemon, ginger, and fresh mint

A Moroccan brand of naturally carbonated mineral water called Oulmes is a standard beverage that accompanies the other drinks on the table.

ABOUT THE RECIPES

This book is intended to introduce you to simple, well explained recipes, so you (and family or friends) can enjoy the simple pleasure of a finely prepared meal made from scratch.

These recipes are great for any variety of occasions. Special celebrations and holiday dinners tend to call for sweet and savory, like Lamb with Prunes and Almonds in Honey Sauce (page 30), or Roasted Chicken with Green Apples and Green Olives (page 70). Some of my favorites for large gatherings with family and friends include Roasted Chicken Thighs with Preserved Lemon and Raisins (page 80), Spicy Baked Fish in Harissa Tomato Sauce with Olives (page 110), or Artichoke Hearts and Green Peas with Garlic and Cilantro (page 138) for a vegetarian option.

But the day-to-day recipes I love for easy family dinners or last-minute meals are things like Merguez in Roasted Bell Pepper and Tomato Sauce with Chermoula (page 58), which can cover breakfast, lunch, and dinner, Chicken Meatballs with Roasted Garlic, Onion, and Parsley (page 74), or Fava Beans with Eggs (page 165).

TIPS

Each recipe in this book contains a tip at the end with additional information that is valuable for your tagine experience:

◇ **Cooking Tip:** Advice on a cooking technique or a labor- or time-saving shortcut.

◇ **Ingredient Tip:** Information about a specific ingredient, where to get it, or how to make it yourself.

◇ **Make Ahead:** Tips for prepping components or even the entire recipe ahead to save time.

◇ **Serving Tip:** Side dishes, condiments, and toppings that will enhance the recipe.

◇ **Storage Tip:** The method and timing for storing the recipe safely with minimal loss of flavor or texture.

◇ **Variation:** Ideas for changing the flavor or base of a recipe or suggestions for what to use if a particular ingredient is unavailable.

CHAPTER 2

LAMB AND BEEF

◄ **Lamb with Butternut Squash Marmalade and Sesame Seeds, 36**

Lamb with Caramelized Onions, Raisins, and Pine Nuts

SERVES 4

PREP TIME:
15 minutes,
plus
20 minutes
or up to
overnight to
marinate

COOK TIME:
3 hours

Sweet and spicy, this tagine is a savory combination of meat stewed in an earthy mix of spices, golden raisins, and sweet caramelized onions. The toasted pine nut garnish is the perfect flavorful finish. You can replace the pine nuts with any nut, such as cashews or almonds, but don't omit them completely because the added crunch breaks up the sweetness of the raisins. This tagine is not an everyday dinner meal; it is a company dish for guests and special occasions. Complete the meal with a garlicky, lemony vegetable side dish.

1 tablespoon Karima's Lamb Spice Mix (page 178)

¾ teaspoon ras el hanout, homemade (page 15) or store-bought

¾ cup water, divided

3 pounds bone-in lamb shoulder or leg, cut into 3-inch pieces by the butcher

1 teaspoon kosher salt

2 tablespoons extra-virgin olive oil, plus more for greasing the tagine

3 small yellow onions, 2 cut into ⅓-inch slices and 1 cut into thin half-moons

Boiling water

1 cup packed golden raisins

¼ teaspoon ground cinnamon

1 tablespoon unsalted butter, melted

¼ teaspoon smen, ghee, or melted butter (optional)

¼ cup toasted pine nuts, for serving

1. In a small bowl, mix the lamb spice mix, ras el hanout, and ¼ cup of water to make a thin paste.

2. Place the lamb chunks in a large bowl and rub them all over with the salt. Add 3 tablespoons of the spice paste and toss to coat the meat. Cover the meat and marinate in the refrigerator for 20 minutes or up to overnight. Cover the bowl with the remaining spice paste and refrigerate as well.

3. Grease the inside of the tagine base with olive oil. Arrange the onion slices in two layers, then arrange the marinated pieces of lamb, working from the center out, leaving a 1-inch border around the edges. Lay the half-moon onions around the edges.

4. Add ¼ cup of water and 2 tablespoons of olive oil to the spice paste and mix well. Pour the spice mixture evenly over the meat and onions.

5. Add the remaining ½ cup of water to the bowl that held the spice paste and swirl around. Slowly pour the water around the edges of the tagine.

6. Cover the tagine, place it on a diffuser over low heat, and cook for about 3 hours, or until the meat is tender, the liquid is reduced by half, and the onions are caramelized. Check the liquid level every hour and add boiling water as needed.

7. In the last hour, spread the raisins on top of the meat and onions, sprinkle with cinnamon, and drizzle with the smen (if using). Serve garnished with the toasted pine nuts.

COOKING TIP: When the only vegetable used in the recipe is onions, be careful not to add too much water because this vegetable releases a lot of liquid as it cooks. Just add water a little at a time, to ensure the onions caramelize.

Lamb with Cauliflower and Preserved Lemon

SERVES 4

PREP TIME:
20 minutes,
plus
20 minutes
to marinate

COOK TIME:
3 hours

This recipe is typically prepared with lamb, but it's also delicious with beef—either a cut such as chuck roast or stew meat. Less olive oil is used when cooking with bone-in meat, so the taste and aroma from the meat and bone stand out. This dish is lovely with Kalamata olives, so add some as a garnish if you desire.

3 tablespoons chopped fresh cilantro, divided

¼ preserved lemon, homemade (page 172) or store-bought, chopped

4 garlic cloves, minced

1 teaspoon kosher salt

1¼ cups water, divided

1 tablespoon Karima's Lamb Spice Mix (page 178)

2 pounds bone-in lamb shoulder or leg, cut into 3-inch pieces by the butcher

2 tablespoons extra-virgin olive oil, divided, plus more for greasing the tagine

2 celery stalks, cut into 2-inch pieces

1 large onion, cut into ⅓-inch-thick slices

1 medium tomato, finely chopped, or ½ cup canned crushed tomatoes

Boiling water

1 medium head cauliflower, broken into large florets, or 1 (10-ounce) bag thawed frozen cauliflower

1. In a small food processor (or using a mortar and pestle), crush 2 tablespoons of cilantro, the preserved lemon, garlic, and salt.

2. In a small bowl, mix ¼ cup of water and the spice mix to make a thin paste.

3. Place the lamb chunks in a large bowl and add the preserved lemon mixture and 3 tablespoons of the spice paste, tossing to coat the meat. Cover the meat and marinate in the refrigerator for 15 to 20 minutes. Cover the bowl with the remaining spice paste and refrigerate.

4. Grease the inside of the tagine base with olive oil and lay the celery in the base. Arrange two layers of onion slices on top. Top the onion with the tomato. Add the marinated lamb, working from the center out, leaving a 1½-inch border all around the edges. Drizzle 1 tablespoon of olive oil over the meat and vegetables and pour ½ cup of water slowly around the edges of the tagine.

5. Cover the tagine, place it on a diffuser over medium-low heat, and cook for about 2 hours, checking the liquid level every hour, and adding boiling water as needed.

6. After 2 hours of cooking, pour the remaining ½ cup of water and remaining 1 tablespoon of olive oil into the reserved spice mix.

7. Uncover the tagine carefully, set the cauliflower florets around the meat, and pour the spice mixture evenly over the florets, adjusting the level of water if needed. Cover the tagine and cook for 1 hour, or until the meat is tender, the florets are soft, and the sauce is reduced by half.

8. Set the tagine on a cooling rack to cool for 10 minutes. Serve garnished with the remaining 1 tablespoon of cilantro.

COOKING TIP: Occasionally, scoop the sauce over the cauliflower florets as they cook, so they pick up an appetizing color and the flavor of the meat sauce.

Lamb with Prunes and Almonds in Honey Sauce

Called *m'rouzia* in Arabic, this dish is special in Moroccan cuisine. It is prepared mainly for the holiday of Eid al-Adha, which traditionally is celebrated with the sacrifice of a lamb. Because it is a celebratory dish, it contains only meat, fruits, and sweet sauce but no vegetables, so you need to balance the dish with a savory side like sautéed cabbage or a roasted red pepper and tomato salad. Saffron can be expensive but is fitting for this holiday dish, and adds an ineffable flavor to this tagine. If you can't come by it, you can leave it out.

1 cup water, divided

2 teaspoons ras el hanout, homemade (page 15) or store-bought

1 teaspoon kosher salt

2 teaspoons Karima's Lamb Spice Mix (page 178)

⅛ teaspoon saffron threads, plus 2 or 3 threads, crumbled

3 pounds bone-in lamb neck or shoulder, cut into 4 pieces

2 tablespoons extra-virgin olive oil, plus more for greasing the tagine

2 medium yellow onions, cut into ⅓-inch-thick slices

¼ teaspoon smen or ghee (optional)

Boiling water

1 cup prunes

1 tablespoon unsalted butter, melted

1 tablespoon honey

1 cup blanched almonds (or any nut you desire), toasted and left whole, sliced, or chopped

1. In a large bowl, mix ¼ cup of water, the ras el hanout, salt, spice mix, and ⅛ teaspoon of saffron to make a thin paste. Add the lamb pieces, toss to coat, cover, and marinate in the refrigerator for 20 minutes or up to overnight.

2. Grease the inside of the tagine base with olive oil and arrange two layers of onion slices. Add the marinated lamb, working from the center out, leaving about 1½ inches of space around the edges.

3. Add ¼ cup of water, 2 tablespoons of olive oil, and the smen (if using) to the marinade bowl, swirl it around, and the pour it evenly over the meat and onions. Pour the remaining ½ cup of water slowly around the edges of the tagine.

4. Cover the tagine, place it on a diffuser over medium-low heat, and cook for about 2 hours. Check the liquid level every hour and add boiling water as needed.

5. While the tagine is cooking, in a small bowl, combine the prunes, ½ cup of boiling water, the melted butter, and remaining 2 or 3 saffron threads and set it aside to soften for 10 minutes.

6. After 2 hours of cooking, uncover the tagine, spread the prunes around and on the meat, pour the liquid from the prune bowl all over, and drizzle with the honey. Cover the tagine and let it finish the cooking, about 1 hour more.

7. Set the tagine on a cooling rack to cool slightly. Serve garnished with the almonds.

INGREDIENT TIP: The cooking time of lamb or any meat varies depending on the animal's age and whether they are grass-fed. If the meat is light in color like baby lamb, it will cook faster.

Lamb in Herbed Tomato and Okra Sauce

SERVES 4

PREP TIME:
15 minutes,
plus
20 minutes
or up to
overnight to
marinate

COOK TIME:
3 hours

Tagine of okra is usually prepared with lamb or beef. This recipe calls for baby okra or young okra, but if you can only get larger, long pods, they should be cut into small pieces. Okra is known for its rows of tiny seeds and slimy or sticky texture when cut open. This sticky substance will naturally thicken any cooking liquid. The taste and texture of okra are unique, and it goes well with tomato sauce, oregano, jalapeños, and preserved lemon.

1 cup water, divided

3 garlic cloves, minced

¼ preserved lemon, homemade (page 172) or store-bought, finely chopped

1 teaspoon kosher salt

½ tablespoon Karima's Lamb Spice Mix (page 178)

2 pounds bone-in lamb shoulder or leg, cut into 3-inch pieces by the butcher

2 tablespoons extra-virgin olive oil, plus more for greasing the tagine

2 medium yellow onions, coarsely chopped

3 medium tomatoes, finely chopped, or 1½ cups canned crushed tomatoes

2 tablespoons chopped fresh cilantro, plus more for garnish

1 teaspoon dried oregano, crumbled

Boiling water

3 cups baby okra (frozen or fresh)

1. In a large bowl, mix ¼ cup of water, the garlic, preserved lemon, salt, and spice mix to make a thin paste. Add the lamb, toss to coat, cover, and marinate in the refrigerator for 20 minutes or up to overnight.

2. Grease the inside of the tagine base with olive oil, arrange the onions in an even layer, then make a layer of tomatoes and top the vegetables with the marinated lamb.

3. In the marinade bowl, stir together the remaining marinade, ¼ cup of water, the olive oil, cilantro, and oregano until well blended. Pour the mixture all over the meat and vegetables. Put the remaining ½ cup of water into the empty bowl, swirl around, and pour the water slowly around the edges of the tagine.

4. Cover the tagine, place it on a diffuser over medium-low heat, and cook for 2 hours. Check the liquid level every hour and add boiling water as needed.

5. After 2 hours, uncover and add the okra. If the sauce is thick, add boiling water to thin it out because okra releases a natural thickener as it cooks. Taste the sauce to adjust the salt, cover the tagine, and let it finish cooking for about 1 hour more, or until the meat is tender, the okra is soft, and the sauce is slightly thickened.

6. Remove the tagine from the heat. Serve garnished with cilantro.

COOKING TIP: Always check and taste the food before serving when you are a beginner. Also, when the recipe says to add water but the tagine has enough water, do not add it because some vegetables do not absorb water.

Lamb with Chickpeas and Turnip

SERVES 4

PREP TIME:
15 minutes,
plus
20 minutes
or up to
overnight to
marinate

COOK TIME:
3 hours

A combination of meat, legumes, and an underused root vegetable (turnip) results in a wonderful one-pot meal for a weekday family dinner. The dish is often prepared in the winter because it's so rich and filling. Add a couple of pieces of pita bread and a chopped vegetable salad to round out the meal.

1 cup water, divided

3 garlic cloves, minced

3 tablespoons chopped fresh cilantro, divided

1 tablespoon Karima's Lamb Spice Mix (page 178)

1 teaspoon kosher salt

¼ teaspoon saffron threads, crumbled

2 pounds bone-in lamb shoulder, cut into 3-inch pieces by the butcher, or 1½ pounds boneless, cut into 3-inch pieces

2 tablespoons extra-virgin olive oil, plus more for greasing the tagine

4 sprigs fresh parsley

1 large yellow onion, cut into ⅓-inch-thick slices

2 cups dried chickpeas (soaked overnight), or canned chickpeas, drained and rinsed

Boiling water

3 small turnips, peeled and quartered

Fluffy Couscous (page 170), brown or white rice, or quinoa, for serving

1. In a large bowl, mix ¼ cup of water, the garlic, 2 tablespoons of cilantro, the spice mix, salt, and saffron until well combined. Add the lamb, toss to coat, cover, and marinate in the refrigerator for 20 minutes or up to overnight.

2. Grease the inside of the tagine base with olive oil and arrange the parsley sprigs across the base. Arrange the sliced onion in an even layer over the herbs and top with the lamb, reserving the remaining marinade.

3. If using soaked chickpeas, add them on top of the meat at this point because they need more time to cook than canned chickpeas. Add ¼ cup of water and the 2 tablespoons of olive oil to the reserved marinade and mix well. Pour it evenly over the meat, chickpeas, and onion. Put the remaining ½ cup of water into the empty bowl, swirl around, and pour it slowly around the edges of the tagine.

4. Cover the tagine, place it on a diffuser over medium-low heat, and cook for 2 hours. Check the liquid level every hour and add boiling water as needed.

5. After 2 hours of cooking, if using canned chickpeas, add them now with the turnips, piling them up in a conical shape and fully covering the meat. Baste the sauce over the turnips a few times. Cover the tagine and cook for about 1 hour, or until the meat is tender, the chickpeas and turnips are soft, and the sauce is reduced by half.

6. Set the tagine on a cooling rack to cool for 10 minutes. Serve garnished with the remaining 1 tablespoon of cilantro. Serve this dish over couscous, brown or white rice, or quinoa.

COOKING TIP: For food safety reasons, after adding a marinade that has had raw meat in it to the tagine, always wait until it has cooked for 1½ hours before tasting and adjusting the seasoning.

Lamb with Butternut Squash Marmalade and Sesame Seeds

SERVES 4

PREP TIME:
15 minutes,
plus
20 minutes
or up to
overnight to
marinate

COOK TIME:
3 hours

Here is a sweet and savory tagine for butternut squash lovers. It is an old Berber specialty of the Middle Atlas area—a mountain range in Morocco. It is not a popular dish, but it is special for me because this recipe was my mom's favorite. The vibrant color of the butternut squash and the crunch of sesame seeds makes it the ideal special-occasion meal. Try it with a nice piece of veal or beef if lamb is unavailable.

1 cup water, divided

1 teaspoon kosher salt, plus a pinch

¾ teaspoon ras el hanout, homemade (page 15) or store-bought, plus a pinch

2 teaspoons Karima's Lamb Spice Mix (page 178)

⅛ teaspoon saffron threads, crumbled

2 pounds bone-in lamb leg, cut into 3-inch pieces by the butcher

3 tablespoons extra-virgin olive oil, divided, plus more for greasing the tagine

2 medium yellow onions, cut into ⅓-inch-thick slices

Boiling water

1 pound butternut squash cubes (1-inch), fresh or frozen

½ teaspoon grated lemon zest

1 tablespoon freshly squeezed lemon juice

1 or 2 tablespoons honey, plus more (optional) as desired

1 tablespoon unsalted butter, melted

2 tablespoons toasted sesame seeds

1. In a small bowl, mix ¼ cup of water, the salt, ras el hanout, spice mix, and saffron to make a thin paste. Place the meat in a medium bowl, add 3 tablespoons of the spice mixture, and toss to coat. Marinate the meat in the refrigerator for 20 minutes or up to overnight. Cover and refrigerate the remaining spice paste.

2. Grease the inside of the tagine base with olive oil and arrange the sliced onions in two layers in the base. Top the onions with the marinated meat. Add ¼ cup of water and 2 tablespoons of olive oil to the marinade left in the bowl and drizzle the mixture over the meat and onions evenly. Put the remaining ½ cup of water into the empty bowl, swirl it around, and pour it slowly around the edges of the tagine.

3. Cover the tagine and set it on a diffuser over low heat, and cook for 2 hours. Check the liquid level every hour and add boiling water as needed.

4. While the tagine cooks, in a medium bowl, toss the butternut squash with the remaining 1 tablespoon of olive oil, a pinch of ras el hanout, a pinch of salt, the lemon zest, and lemon juice. Drizzle the honey over the squash cubes and toss gently.

5. After 2 hours of cooking, uncover the tagine and arrange the butternut squash cubes on the top of the meat. Cover the tagine again and let it cook for about 1 hour longer, or until the meat is very soft, the onions are caramelized, and the sauce is reduced.

6. Use a fork to smash the squash cubes into the meat mixture gently and drizzle with the melted butter and more honey (if desired). Serve garnished with the sesame seeds.

SERVING TIP: This tagine is best served over Fluffy Couscous (page 170) or with bread such as French baguette or homemade Tagine Baked Bread (page 168) made with anise seeds and sesame seeds.

Lamb in Sweet and Savory Sauce with Fennel and Dried Figs

SERVES 4

PREP TIME:
15 minutes,
plus
20 minutes
or up to
overnight to
marinate

COOK TIME:
3 hours

The aroma of the spices and meat, combined with the fennel's enticing licorice flavor and natural sweetness from the figs, creates a spectacular tagine. If the flavor of fennel is not your favorite, don't fret; it becomes less intense and sweeter when cooked. This sweet and savory meal is best served with spicy olives or a side dish of vegetables with harissa.

1 cup water, divided

3 garlic cloves, minced

¼ preserved lemon, homemade (page 172) or store-bought, finely chopped

3 tablespoons chopped fresh cilantro, divided

1 teaspoon kosher salt, or more as desired

½ teaspoon ras el hanout, homemade (page 15) or store-bought

2 teaspoons Karima's Lamb Spice Mix (page 178)

2 pounds bone-in lamb leg, cut into 3-inch pieces by the butcher

2 tablespoons extra-virgin olive oil, plus more for greasing the tagine

2 celery stalks, cut into 2-inch pieces

1 large yellow onion, cut into ⅓-inch-thick slices

Boiling water

3 fennel bulbs, trimmed, halved through the stem, and cut into 1-inch wedges

12 small dried figs

1. In a large bowl, mix ¼ cup of water, the garlic, preserved lemon, 2 tablespoons of cilantro, the salt, ras el hanout, and spice mix until well combined. Add the meat and toss to coat. Marinate the meat in the refrigerator for 20 minutes or up to overnight.

2. Grease the inside of the tagine base with olive oil and arrange the celery pieces across the base. Top the celery with two layers of sliced onion, then the lamb pieces.

3. Add ¼ cup of water to the reserved marinade and mix well. Pour it evenly over the meat and vegetables. Put the remaining ½ cup of water into the empty bowl, swirl around, and pour it slowly around the edges of the tagine.

4. Cover the tagine, place it on a diffuser over medium-low heat, and cook for 2 hours. Check the liquid level every hour and add boiling water as needed.

5. After 2 hours of cooking, arrange the fennel wedges on the meat, piling them up in a conical shape, and place the figs all around the fennel. Baste the sauce over the fennel and figs a few times.

6. Cover the tagine and cook for about 1 hour more, or until the meat is tender, the vegetables and fruit are soft, and the sauce is reduced by half.

7. Set the tagine on a cooling rack to cool for 10 minutes. Serve garnished with the remaining 1 tablespoon of cilantro.

VARIATION: If figs aren't to your taste, you can swap them for another dried fruit. The same is true for the fennel; you can swap it for the vegetable of your choice. Or make the dish savory by using green peas and green olives instead of figs.

Beef with Zucchini and Oregano

SERVES 6

PREP TIME:
20 minutes,
plus
20 minutes
or up to
overnight to
marinate

COOK TIME:
3 hours

An earthy savory dish very common in Morocco, this tagine uses vibrant green zucchini—which in Morocco are called courgettes. Mild flavored zucchini with its edible skin, combined with the flavorful spices, preserved lemon, and earthy oregano, makes a well-balanced, tasty meal with a beautiful finish in the end.

¾ cup water, divided

4 tablespoons chopped fresh cilantro, divided

6 garlic cloves, minced

¼ small preserved lemon, homemade (page 172) or store-bought, finely chopped

1 teaspoon kosher salt

½ tablespoon Karima's Beef Spice Mix (page 177)

2 pounds bone-in beef chuck or rump, cut into 4-inch pieces by the butcher

2 tablespoons extra-virgin olive oil, plus more for greasing the tagine

2 medium yellow onions, cut into ⅓-inch-thick slices

2 medium tomatoes, chopped, or 1 cup canned crushed tomatoes

Boiling water

1½ pounds medium zucchini, quartered crosswise

1 teaspoon dried oregano, crumbled

1. In a small bowl, mix ¼ cup of water, 2 tablespoons of cilantro, the garlic, preserved lemon, salt, and spice mix to make a thin paste. Place the beef in a medium bowl, add ¼ cup of the spice mixture, and toss to coat. Cover and marinate the meat in the refrigerator for 20 minutes or up to overnight. Cover and refrigerate the remaining spice paste.

2. Grease the inside of the tagine base with olive oil and arrange the sliced onions in two layers. Layer the tomatoes on the onions and top with the marinated meat, working from the center out. Drizzle everything with 1 tablespoon of

olive oil. Put the remaining ½ cup of water into the empty marinade bowl, swirl around, and pour it slowly around the edges of the tagine.

3. Cover the tagine and set it on a diffuser over medium-low heat, and cook for 2 hours. Check the liquid level every hour and add boiling water as needed.

4. After 2 hours of cooking, uncover the tagine and arrange the zucchini on the top of the meat in a conical shape. To the reserved spice paste, add ¼ cup of boiling water and the remaining 1 tablespoon of olive oil and mix well. Pour the mixture over the whole dish, and sprinkle with the oregano. Cover the tagine and cook for about 1 hour longer, or until the meat is very tender.

5. Set the tagine on a cooling rack to cool for 10 minutes. Serve garnished with the remaining 2 tablespoons of cilantro.

COOKING TIP: If the meat used is fatty, reduce the amount of olive oil. You can adjust the amount as needed before the dish is completely cooked.

Beef Shank with Green Peas and Artichoke Hearts

SERVES 4

PREP TIME:
25 minutes,
plus
20 minutes
to marinate

COOK TIME:
3½ hours

A common spring dish in Morocco, this lovely tagine is for when peas and artichoke hearts are in season, although it can be made year-round using frozen veggies. I remember my mom calling me and my siblings to help her snip off the spiky leaf tops and meaty ends of the artichokes, so she could easily trim them down to the hearts. We helped with the fresh green peas, too, but we ate so many of them raw that the tagine had none! It takes time to clean and prepare these fresh vegetables for cooking, but trust me, it is well worth it for a tasty, incredibly flavorful, and healthy dish.

¾ cup water, divided

¼ preserved lemon, homemade (page 172) or store-bought, finely chopped, plus 2 tablespoons finely chopped, for garnish

4 garlic cloves, minced

2 tablespoons chopped fresh cilantro

1 tablespoon Karima's Beef Spice Mix (page 177)

2 pounds bone-in beef shank, cut into 4 pieces by the butcher, or 1½ pounds boneless beef, cut into 8 pieces

1 teaspoon kosher salt

2 tablespoons extra-virgin olive oil, divided, plus more for greasing the tagine

2 medium yellow onions, cut into ⅓-inch-thick slices

2 medium tomatoes, chopped, or 1 cup canned crushed tomatoes

Boiling water

6 canned water-packed artichoke hearts

1 pound green peas, fresh or frozen

1. In a small bowl, mix ¼ cup of water, the ¼ preserved lemon, garlic, cilantro, and spice mix to make a thin paste. Place the beef in a large bowl and rub the pieces all over with the salt. Add 3 tablespoons of the spice paste and toss to coat. Cover and marinate the meat in the refrigerator for 20 minutes. Set the remaining spice paste aside.

2. Grease the inside of the tagine base with olive oil. Arrange the sliced onions in two layers. Layer the tomatoes and top with the marinated beef, working from the center out. Drizzle 1 tablespoon of olive oil over the meat and vegetables and pour the remaining ½ cup of water slowly around the edges of the tagine.

3. Cover the tagine, place it on a diffuser over medium-low heat, and cook for about 2 hours. Check the liquid level every hour and add boiling water as needed.

4. After 2 hours, take the spice mix out of the refrigerator and stir in ¼ cup of boiling water and the remaining 1 tablespoon of olive oil. Uncover the tagine carefully, and arrange the artichoke hearts around and on top of the meat. Then spread the peas over the meat, covering it. Pour the spice mixture evenly over the whole dish.

5. Cover the tagine and cook for about 1½ hours longer, or until the meat is very soft, the vegetables are tender, and the sauce is reduced by half.

6. Set the tagine on a cooling rack to cool for 10 minutes. Serve garnished with the remaining 2 tablespoons of preserved lemon.

COOKING TIP: If adding boiling water, only add a little at a time, because too much water will take too long to reduce, and you will end up with watery sauce and overcooked food.

Beef with Sweet Potatoes, Apricots, and Almonds

SERVES 4

PREP TIME:
25 minutes,
plus
25 minutes
or up to
overnight to
marinate

COOK TIME:
3 to 4 hours

This dish is naturally sweet from the caramelized onions and roasted sweet potato, savory from marjoram and ras el hanout, and sour from the dried apricots. This combination creates a beautifully balanced meal, especially when served with leafy greens or garlic and spicy side dishes.

¾ cup water, divided

1 teaspoon ras el hanout, homemade (page 15) or store-bought, plus a pinch

1 teaspoon Karima's Beef Spice Mix (page 177)

2 pounds bone-in beef chuck or blade, cut into 3-inch pieces by the butcher, or 1½ pounds boneless, cut into 3-inch pieces

1 teaspoon kosher salt, plus more for sprinkling

2 tablespoons extra-virgin olive oil, divided, plus more for greasing the tagine

2 medium yellow onions, cut into ⅓-inch-thick slices

Boiling water

2 large or 3 medium sweet potatoes, cut crosswise into ⅓-inch-thick rounds

1 teaspoon dried marjoram or 1 tablespoon chopped fresh

½ cup chopped dried apricots

1 tablespoon unsalted butter, melted

½ cup slivered almonds

1. In a small bowl, mix ¼ cup water, the ras el hanout, and spice mix to make a thin paste. Place the beef in a large bowl and rub the pieces all over with the salt. Add 3 tablespoons of the spice paste and toss to coat. Cover and marinate the meat in the refrigerator for 20 to 25 minutes or up to overnight. Cover and refrigerate the remaining spice paste.

2. Grease the inside of the tagine base with olive oil. Arrange the sliced onions in two layers. Layer the marinated beef from the center out, leaving 1½ inches around the edges.

3. In a small bowl, mix ¼ cup of water, 1 tablespoon of olive oil, and the remaining reserved spice paste. Use a large spoon to pour the mixture evenly over the meat and vegetables. Put ¼ cup of water into the empty marinade bowl, swirl around, and slowly pour it around the edges of the tagine.

4. Cover the tagine, place it on a diffuser over medium-low heat, and cook for about 2 hours. Check the liquid level every hour and add boiling water as needed.

5. After 2 hours of cooking, uncover the tagine and arrange the sweet potatoes on top of the meat, covering it. Sprinkle with salt and the marjoram and drizzle the remaining 1 tablespoon of olive oil evenly over the whole dish. Cover the tagine again and cook for about 1 hour longer, or until the meat is very tender, the vegetables are tender, and the sauce reduced.

6. While the tagine is cooking, place the apricots and a pinch of ras el hanout in a medium bowl and cover with 1 cup of boiling water. Soak for 10 minutes, drain, and set them aside for garnish.

7. Preheat the oven to broil and when the tagine is done, remove the lid. Drizzle the melted butter on top and broil for 5 minutes, or until the sweet potatoes are golden. Serve garnished with the apricots and almonds.

MAKE AHEAD: Although a short marinating time will still produce a delicious meal, it is best to marinate overnight.

Braised Lamb Shank with Carrots and Green Beans

SERVES 4

PREP TIME:
20 minutes,
plus
20 minutes
or up to
overnight to
marinate

COOK TIME:
3 to 4 hours

Lamb shank tagine will improve after it marinates overnight in the refrigerator, giving the flavors time to meld and deepen. This dish is a lovely dinner to offer on cold nights. It is best served with spicy olives; beet salad; a Moroccan salad of tomato, cucumber, and red onion; and homemade bread.

1¼ cups water, divided

4 garlic cloves, minced

¼ preserved lemon, homemade (page 172) or store-bought, finely chopped

2 tablespoons chopped fresh cilantro, divided

1 teaspoon kosher salt

2 teaspoons Karima's Lamb Spice Mix (page 178)

4 small lamb shanks (or 2 large shanks cut into 2 pieces by the butcher)

2 tablespoons extra-virgin olive oil, plus more for greasing the tagine

2 medium yellow onions, cut into ⅓-inch-thick slices.

2 medium tomatoes, chopped, or 1 cup canned crushed tomatoes

Boiling water

3 cups halved green beans, fresh or frozen

3 medium carrots, cut into ½-inch-thick sticks

1. In a small bowl, mix together ¼ cup of water, the garlic, preserved lemon, 1 tablespoon of cilantro, the salt, and spice mix to make a thin paste. Place the lamb in a medium bowl, add ¼ cup of the spice mixture, and toss to coat. Cover and marinate the meat in the refrigerator for 20 minutes or up to overnight. Cover and refrigerate the remaining spice paste.

2. Grease the inside of the tagine base with olive oil. Arrange the sliced onions in two layers. Layer the tomatoes and top with the marinated lamb from the center out, leaving about 1½ inches around the edges.

3. Add ½ cup of water and 2 tablespoons of olive oil to the reserved spice paste and mix well. Pour 3 tablespoons of the mixture evenly over the meat and vegetables. Set the remaining mixture aside. Put the remaining ½ cup of water into the empty marinade bowl, swirl, and pour it slowly around the edges of the tagine.

4. Cover the tagine and set it on a diffuser over low heat to cook for 2 hours. Check the liquid level every hour and add boiling water as needed.

5. After 2 hours of cooking, uncover the tagine and arrange the beans and carrots around the shanks, leaving the meat uncovered. Spoon the remaining spice mixture over the vegetables and meat, cover the tagine, and cook for about 1½ hours longer, or until the meat is very tender, the vegetables are tender, and the sauce is reduced by half.

6. Set the tagine on a cooling rack to cool for 10 minutes. Serve garnished with the remaining 1 tablespoon of cilantro.

COOKING TIP: If you cook less fatty meat with less sauce, the top can get dark and look dry. Before adding the vegetables after 2 hours of cooking, use a large flat spoon to flip the pieces of meat over to submerge the dry part in the sauce.

Beef Meatballs in Spicy Tomato Sauce with Eggs

SERVES 4

PREP TIME:
20 minutes

COOK TIME:
50 minutes

A simple combination of meatballs and eggs is a lifesaver when you do not have time to cook and still want to offer something delicious for a weeknight dinner or a casual get-together. This meal is best served with a garlicky, lemony vegetarian side dish, oil-cured black or Kalamata olives, and fresh bread or artisanal French baguette.

1 pound ground beef (90 percent lean)

2 medium yellow or red onions, finely chopped, divided

¼ cup chopped fresh parsley, plus more for garnish

1¼ teaspoons kosher salt, divided

1¼ teaspoons sweet paprika, divided

1¼ teaspoons ground cumin, divided

½ teaspoon cayenne pepper, divided

½ teaspoon freshly ground black pepper

½ teaspoon ground ginger

2 tablespoons extra-virgin olive oil, plus more for greasing the tagine

4 large tomatoes, finely chopped, or 1 (15-ounce) can crushed tomatoes

4 garlic cloves, minced

½ teaspoon dried thyme or oregano

Boiling water

6 large eggs

1. In a large bowl, combine the ground beef, half of the chopped onion, the parsley, 1 teaspoon of salt, 1 teaspoon of paprika, 1 teaspoon of cumin, ¼ teaspoon of cayenne, the black pepper, and ginger. Shape the meat mixture into 2-inch meatballs and set them aside. If you have time, make the meatballs a few hours ahead to overnight, so the meat absorbs all the flavors from the spices.

2. Grease the inside of the tagine base with olive oil. Arrange the remaining chopped onion, the tomatoes, and garlic in the base. Sprinkle with 2 tablespoons of olive oil, the thyme, and the remaining ¼ teaspoon each of salt, paprika, cumin, and cayenne and stir to combine. Add the meatballs to the sauce and spread some of the sauce over them.

3. Cover the tagine and set it on a diffuser over low heat to cook for 40 minutes, or until the meatballs are firm but juicy and the tomato sauce is thick. Check after 20 minutes and add boiling water as needed.

4. After 40 minutes, uncover the tagine and crack the eggs between the meatballs, leaving space between them. Cover the tagine and cook the eggs for 5 to 7 minutes, until the whites are set.

5. Set the tagine on a cooling rack to cool for 10 minutes. Serve garnished with parsley.

MAKE AHEAD: Most of the prep can be done the night before, except chopping the onions, which is best done close to the cooking time or just a little before, so they stay fresh and juicy. Add less olive oil to the tomato sauce if you use ground beef with more fat; you can always adjust it afterward.

Ground Lamb Kebabs with Onion, Cabbage, and Carrots

SERVES 4

PREP TIME:
25 minutes

COOK TIME:
1 hour
20 minutes

Here is another easy dish that will not take a lot of your time and looks very satisfying on your dinner table. It makes a light meal with a nice combination of onions, cabbage, and carrots infused with the tasty juices from well-seasoned lamb meatballs. This dish is best served with olives, or a refreshing cumin-roasted bell pepper and tomato salad.

1 pound ground lamb

2 yellow onions, 1 finely chopped and 1 halved and cut into ⅓-inch-thick slices

6 tablespoons chopped fresh parsley, plus 2 tablespoons

2 teaspoons ras el hanout, homemade (page 15) or store-bought

2 teaspoons ground cumin, divided

1½ teaspoons sweet paprika, divided

1¼ teaspoons kosher salt, divided

1 teaspoon harissa, homemade (page 174) or store-bought, divided

4 garlic cloves, minced

1 tablespoon extra-virgin olive oil, plus more for greasing the tagine

3 cups thickly sliced green cabbage

2 cups sliced carrots

¼ cup water

Boiling water

1. In a large bowl, combine the ground lamb, chopped onion, 6 tablespoons of parsley, the ras el hanout, 1 teaspoon of cumin, 1 teaspoon of paprika, 1 teaspoon of salt, and ½ teaspoon of harissa until well combined. Add 1 teaspoon of water if needed to make a firm mixture. Shape the meat mixture into 3-inch-long cigar shapes and set them aside. If you have time, make the kebabs a few hours ahead to overnight, so the meat can absorb all the flavors from the spices.

2. In a small bowl, mix the garlic, remaining 1 teaspoon of cumin, ½ teaspoon of paprika, and remaining ½ teaspoon of harissa. (If the mixture is too thick, add 1 or 2 tablespoons of water.) Set aside.

3. Grease the inside of the tagine base with olive oil. Arrange the onion slices in an even layer in the base. Top the onions with layers of cabbage and carrots and sprinkle with the remaining ¼ teaspoon of salt. Pour the reserved harissa mixture over the vegetables.

4. Pour ¼ cup of water slowly around the edges of the tagine and drizzle everything with the 1 tablespoon of olive oil.

5. Cover the tagine and set it on a diffuser over medium-low heat to cook for 30 to 40 minutes, until the cabbage and carrots soften. Check the liquid level every 15 minutes and add boiling water as needed.

6. After 30 minutes of cooking, uncover the tagine and arrange the lamb kebabs on the vegetables. Cover the tagine, reduce the heat to low, and cook for another 30 to 40 minutes, until the kebabs are firm but soft and juicy inside and the vegetables are lightly caramelized.

7. Remove the tagine from the heat. Serve garnished with the remaining 2 tablespoons of parsley.

COOKING TIP: Ground beef or lamb can be overcooked easily, especially in a tagine. Make sure you take the tagine off the heat in time because the ground meat will keep cooking as the tagine stays hot for a while.

Beef Stew with Green Apples, Raisins, and Toasted Sesame Seeds

SERVES 4

PREP TIME:
15 minutes,
plus
15 minutes
or up to
overnight to
marinate

COOK TIME:
2 hours

Make this beef tagine when apples are in season. The sweet and savory combination of sweet raisins, tart apple, and spiced beef create a deep, rich flavor.

½ cup water, plus 2 tablespoons

2 teaspoons Karima's Beef Spice Mix (page 177)

1 teaspoon kosher salt, plus more as desired

1 teaspoon ras el hanout, homemade (page 15) or store-bought

⅛ teaspoon saffron threads, crumbled, plus a few extra threads

1½ pounds boneless beef chuck, cut into 2-inch pieces

2 tablespoons extra-virgin olive oil, plus more for greasing the tagine

2 medium yellow onions, cut into ½-inch chunks

Boiling water

3 large green apples, cored and cut into sixths

1 cup loosely packed golden raisins

2 tablespoons unsalted butter, melted

1 to 2 tablespoons honey, as desired

1 tablespoon toasted sesame seeds, for garnish

1. In a medium bowl, mix 2 tablespoons of water, the spice mix, salt, ras el hanout, and saffron to make a thin paste. Add the beef and turn to coat. Cover and marinate the meat for 15 minutes or up to overnight in the refrigerator.

2. Grease the inside of the tagine base with olive oil. Arrange the onion chunks in a layer in the base and place the marinated beef on top. Put ¼ cup of water into the empty marinade bowl, swirl, and spoon the mixture evenly over everything. Drizzle the 2 tablespoons olive oil over the meat

and vegetables and pour the remaining ¼ cup of water slowly around the edges of the tagine.

3. Cover the tagine, place it on a diffuser over medium-low heat, and cook for 1½ hours, or until the meat is tender. Check the liquid level every 45 minutes and add boiling water as needed.

4. After 1½ hours of cooking, uncover the tagine and arrange the apples on top of the meat in concentric circles, like a tart. Sprinkle with the raisins, drizzle with the melted butter, sprinkle on a few saffron threads, and drizzle with the honey. Cover the tagine and cook for about 30 minutes longer, or until the meat is very tender, the apple is tender but not mushy, and the sauce is reduced by half.

5. Set the tagine on a cooling rack to cool for 10 minutes. Serve garnished with sesame seeds.

STORAGE TIP: Always store the tagine pot at room temperature or in a warm place to extend its life. Exposing the pot to hot and cold temperatures can weaken it over time.

Beef Stew with Seven Vegetables

SERVES 4

PREP TIME:
15 minutes,
plus
20 minutes
to marinate

COOK TIME:
3 hours

The most frequently prepared meal in Moroccan households on Friday, this traditional tagine is so special! It is a delightful beef stew with seven vegetables, which should be served on Fluffy Couscous (page 170) so the flavorful, aromatic broth can soak right in. This stew is often cooked in a deep clay pot with a steamer on the top for the couscous, but it will work in the tagine as a small meal.

¾ cup water, divided

1 teaspoon ras el hanout, homemade (page 15) or store-bought

¾ teaspoon Karima's Beef Spice Mix (page 177)

2 pounds bone-in beef blade or chuck, cut into 3-inch pieces by the butcher

1½ teaspoons kosher salt, divided

3 tablespoons extra-virgin olive oil, divided, plus more for greasing the tagine

1 medium yellow onion, cut into ⅓-inch-thick slices

1 medium tomato, finely chopped, or ½ cup canned crushed tomatoes

Boiling water

1 cup canned chickpeas, drained and rinsed

¼ small head cabbage, cut into ¼-inch wedges

2 medium carrots, cut into thick sticks

1 small turnip, quartered

2 small zucchini, halved lengthwise

4 (1-inch) slices peeled butternut squash

1. In a small bowl, mix ¼ cup of water, the ras el hanout, and spice mix to make a thin paste. Place the beef in a large bowl and rub the pieces all over with 1 teaspoon of salt. Add 3 tablespoons of the spice paste and toss to coat. Cover and marinate the meat for 20 minutes in the refrigerator. Set the remaining spice paste aside.

2. Grease the inside of the tagine base with olive oil. Arrange the onion slices in an even layer across the base. Arrange the tomato on the onion and top with the marinated beef, working from the center out. Drizzle the beef and vegetables with 2 tablespoons of olive oil and put the remaining ½ cup of water into the empty marinade bowl, swirl, and slowly pour it around the edges of the tagine.

3. Cover the tagine, place it on a diffuser over medium-low heat, and cook for 2 hours. Check the liquid level every hour and add boiling water as needed.

4. After 2 hours of cooking, add ½ cup of boiling water, the remaining 1 tablespoon of olive oil, and remaining ½ teaspoon of salt to the reserved spice mixture and mix well. Uncover the tagine and arrange the chickpeas, cabbage, carrots, turnip, zucchini, and butternut squash in layers on top of the meat. Pour the spice mixture evenly over the whole dish.

5. Add ½ cup of boiling water around the edges of the tagine, cover, and cook for about 1 hour longer, or until the meat is very tender, the vegetables are tender, and the sauce is reduced.

6. Set the tagine on a cooling rack to cool for 10 minutes.

SERVING TIP: Serve with a crusty baguette or rustic bread.

Beef with Herbed Garlic-Stuffed Potatoes in Harissa Sauce

SERVES 4

PREP TIME:
25 minutes

COOK TIME:
1 hour
40 minutes

Stuffed vegetables are very common in the Middle East. Stuffed zucchini, eggplant, potatoes, peppers, and tomatoes are popular choices in Moroccan cuisine. Vegetables are filled with various stuffings, ranging from vegetarian rice and herbs to ground meat fillings, and cooked in a spicy, herb-packed tomato sauce.

3 large baking potatoes, halved lengthwise

½ pound ground beef (90 percent lean)

½ cup chopped bell pepper (any color)

½ cup chopped pitted green olives, plus 1 tablespoon

1 large yellow onion, finely chopped

3 tablespoons chopped fresh parsley

2 teaspoons Karima's Beef Spice Mix (page 177)

1¼ teaspoons kosher salt, divided, plus more for seasoning the potatoes

1 teaspoon sweet paprika

1 teaspoon ground cumin

4 tablespoons extra-virgin olive oil, plus more for greasing the tagine and brushing the potatoes

4 large tomatoes, grated, or 2 (15-ounce) cans crushed tomatoes

3 tablespoons chopped fresh cilantro, divided

1 teaspoon dried thyme or oregano

1 teaspoon harissa, homemade (page 174) or store-bought

4 Roasted Garlic (page 173) cloves

Boiling water

1. Using a small spoon, carefully scoop out the flesh of the potato halves, leaving ¼ inch of flesh and intact skin. Submerge the potato halves in a large bowl filled with cold water to prevent them from oxidizing and set them aside.

2. In a large bowl, mix the ground beef, 2 tablespoons of water, the bell pepper, ½ cup of olives, 3 tablespoons

of onion, the parsley, spice mix, 1 teaspoon of salt, the paprika, and cumin and mix well.

3. In a large skillet, heat 2 tablespoons of olive oil over medium-high heat. Add the beef mixture and sauté for 5 to 7 minutes. It does not have to be cooked through because it will continue to cook in the tagine. Remove the skillet from the heat and set it aside to cool for 10 minutes. Use a spoon to break up the mixture while it cools.

4. Grease the inside of the tagine base with olive oil. Add the tomatoes, 2 tablespoons of cilantro, the thyme, harissa, and remaining 2 tablespoons of olive oil, remaining onion, and remaining ¼ teaspoon of salt and mix well.

5. Take the potato halves from the water, blot them dry with paper towels, brush them inside and outside with olive oil, and season them with salt. Evenly divide the meat mixture among the potato halves and place them in the sauce in the tagine. Add the roasted garlic to the sauce and use a spoon to scoop tomato sauce over the potatoes.

6. Cover the tagine, place it on a diffuser over medium-low heat, and cook for about 1½ hours, or until the potatoes soften and the tomato sauce thickens slightly. Check the liquid level every 30 minutes and add boiling water as needed.

7. Set the tagine on a cooling rack to cool for 7 minutes. Serve garnished with the remaining 1 tablespoon of cilantro and 1 tablespoon of olives.

MAKE AHEAD: Components of this dish can be made ahead, such as the tomato sauce. The potatoes should be prepared right when you plan to cook this meal.

Merguez in Roasted Bell Pepper and Tomato Sauce with Chermoula

PREP TIME:
25 minutes

COOK TIME:
1 hour
5 minutes

Merguez is a lamb or lamb and beef sausage that is intensely spiced with harissa, toasted cumin, and coriander. It is very popular and used in many dishes, such as legume stews, sautéed vegetables, or tomato sauce with eggs for a hearty breakfast. This tagine in a roasted pepper and tomato sauce with chermoula is savory, smoky, and easy to prepare for a hearty dinner.

2 tablespoons extra-virgin olive oil, plus more for greasing the tagine

½ medium yellow onion, finely chopped

4 large tomatoes, finely chopped or grated, or 2 (15-ounce) cans crushed tomatoes

2 large roasted red peppers, chopped

⅓ cup chermoula, homemade (page 175) or store-bought

1 tablespoon tomato paste

½ teaspoon dried thyme or oregano

½ teaspoon harissa, homemade (page 174) or store-bought

8 medium merguez sausage links (about 2 ounces each) or any other kind of sausage

Boiling water

1 tablespoon chopped fresh parsley

¼ teaspoon ground cumin

1. Grease the inside of the tagine base with olive oil. Add the onion, tomatoes, roasted peppers, chermoula paste, 2 tablespoons of olive oil, the tomato paste, thyme, and harissa and mix everything well.

2. Nestle the sausage in the sauce and wipe any sauce splashes from the sides of the tagine.

3. Cover the tagine, place it on a diffuser over medium-low heat, and cook for 45 minutes, or until the sausage is cooked and firm to the touch and the sauce is reduced by half. Check the liquid level every 30 minutes and add boiling water as needed.

4. Set the tagine on a cooling rack to cool for 10 minutes. Serve garnished with the parsley and cumin.

SERVING TIP: If you add eggs to this easy dish, you can serve it for brunch or breakfast.

Vegetables Stuffed with Ground Beef

SERVES 4

PREP TIME:
30 minutes

COOK TIME:
1 hour
10 minutes

A make-ahead dish that can be assembled and refrigerated for up to 3 days, this is a perfect last-minute meal or tasty side dish. This tagine is lovely with Moroccan bread, a rustic loaf of bread, or over rice. Although I often stuff the vegetables with just a rice mixture, I also enjoy this delicious and satisfying meat-filled version.

1 pound ground beef (90 percent lean)

½ cup chopped fresh spinach

½ cup finely chopped green cabbage

1 large yellow onion, finely chopped

¼ cup chopped fresh parsley

2½ teaspoons sweet paprika, divided

2½ teaspoons ground cumin, divided

1¼ teaspoons kosher salt, divided, plus more for sprinkling

1 teaspoon ground coriander

3 tablespoons extra-virgin olive oil, divided, plus more for greasing the tagine

1 medium eggplant

1 large zucchini

1 large firm tomato

1 large red bell pepper

4 large tomatoes, finely chopped, or 2 (15-ounce) cans crushed tomatoes

3 tablespoons chopped fresh cilantro, divided

3 garlic cloves, minced

2 teaspoons harissa, homemade (page 174) or store-bought

1 teaspoon dried oregano

Boiling water

6 tablespoons grated mozzarella cheese

1. In a large bowl, mix the ground beef, spinach, cabbage, 3 tablespoons of onion, the parsley, 2 teaspoons of paprika, 2 teaspoons of cumin, 1 teaspoon of salt, and the coriander.

2. In a large skillet, heat 2 tablespoons of olive oil over medium-high heat. Add the beef mixture and sauté for 5 to 7 minutes. It does not have to be cooked through because it will continue to cook in the tagine. Remove the skillet from the heat and set it aside to cool for 10 minutes. Use a spoon to break up the mixture while it cools.

3. Halve the eggplant lengthwise and scoop out the flesh, leaving a ¼-inch wall. Halve the zucchini lengthwise and do the same. Halve the firm tomato and do the same. (The scooped-out flesh can be refrigerated and used in another recipe.) Halve the bell pepper through the stem and pull out the seeds.

4. Sprinkle the hollowed-out vegetables with salt. Carefully fill each of the vegetable halves with the meat filling without breaking them.

5. Grease the inside of the tagine base with olive oil. Add the chopped tomatoes, 2 tablespoons of cilantro, remaining onion, remaining 1 tablespoon of olive oil, the garlic, harissa, oregano, and remaining ½ teaspoon of paprika, ½ teaspoon of cumin, and ¼ teaspoon of salt and stir to mix well. Arrange all the stuffed vegetables in the sauce and spoon some of the tomato sauce on each half.

6. Cover the tagine, place it on a diffuser over medium-low heat, and cook for about 1 hour, or until all the vegetables are soft, the ground beef is cooked, and the tomato sauce is thickened. Check the liquid level every 30 minutes and add boiling water as needed.

continued

Vegetables Stuffed with Ground Beef continued

7. In the last 10 minutes of cooking, uncover the tagine, sprinkle the stuffed vegetables with mozzarella, cover, and continue cooking to melt the cheese, about 5 minutes.

8. When the tagine is done cooking, remove it from the heat and serve topped with the remaining 1 tablespoon of cilantro.

COOKING TIP: You can sauté the beef in the tagine a few hours before stuffing the vegetables, so the meat cools off, and the tagine will collect all the delicious beef cooking aromas.

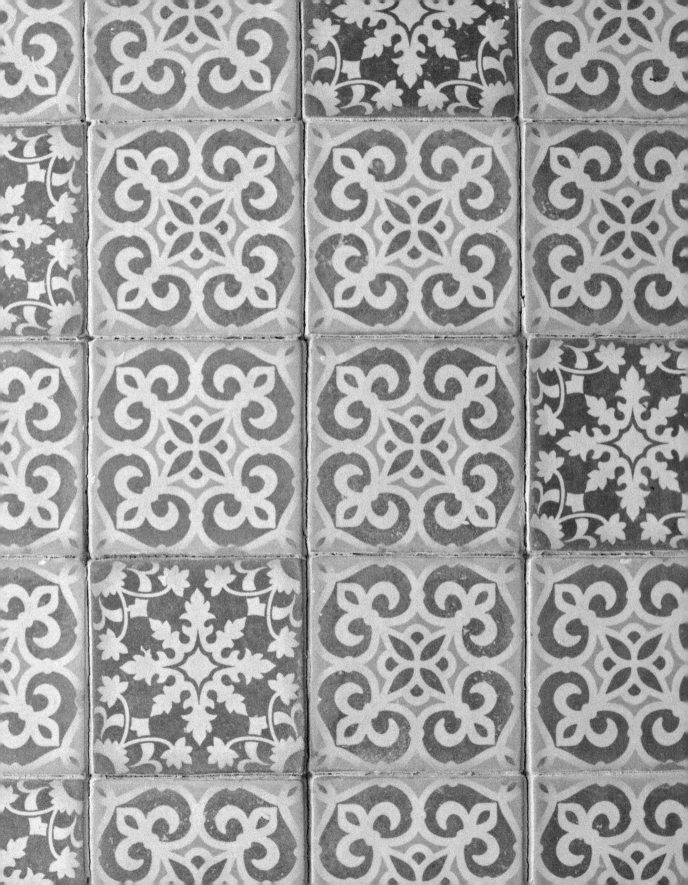

CHAPTER 3

POULTRY

◄ **Duck with Caramelized Onions, Carrots, and Orange, 82**

Chicken with Preserved Lemon, Potato, and Green Olives

SERVES 4

PREP TIME:
15 minutes,
plus
15 minutes
or up to
overnight to
marinate

COOK TIME:
1 hour
30 minutes

A very popular comfort food in Moroccan cuisine, this chicken dish is an easy one to cook in a tagine, with less work and less time than in a pot on the stove. The preserved lemon and ras el hanout are the stars of this meal; the aroma from spices and bold deep citrus flavor of preserved lemon makes it delicious and unique.

½ cup Karima's Chicken Spice Mix (page 178)

¼ preserved lemon, homemade (page 172) or store-bought, chopped, plus 1 tablespoon chopped

1 teaspoon kosher salt

½ teaspoon ras el hanout, homemade (page 15) or store-bought

1 whole chicken (3 pounds), cut into 6 or 8 serving pieces

3 tablespoons extra-virgin olive oil, plus more for greasing the tagine

1 large yellow onion, cut into ⅓-inch-thick slices

6 medium red potatoes, peeled and halved

1 cup pitted green olives

½ cup water

Boiling water

1 tablespoon chopped fresh parsley, for garnish

1. In a large bowl, mix the spice mix, preserved lemon, salt, and ras el hanout into a thin paste. Add the chicken, toss to coat, cover, and marinate for 15 minutes or up to overnight in the refrigerator.

2. Grease the inside of the tagine base with olive oil. Arrange the onion in an even layer in the base and top with the chicken pieces from the center out, leaving 1½ inches around the edges. Arrange the potatoes around the chicken and scatter the olives over everything.

3. Put the water into the empty marinade bowl, swirl, and pour it slowly on the top of the potatoes and around the edges of the tagine. Drizzle the 3 tablespoons of olive oil over the chicken and potatoes.

4. Cover the tagine, place it on a diffuser over low heat, and cook for 1½ hours, or until the chicken is cooked through (internal temperature of 165°F), the potatoes are tender, and the sauce is thick. Check the liquid level every 45 minutes and add boiling water as needed.

5. Set the tagine on a cooling rack to cool for 10 minutes. Serve garnished with the remaining 1 tablespoon of preserved lemon and the parsley.

COOKING TIP: I choose to leave the skin on the chicken because its fat keeps the meat underneath moist and adds more flavor.

Royal Chicken with Caramelized Onions, Raisins, and Almonds

SERVES 4

PREP TIME:
15 minutes,
plus
20 minutes
or up to
overnight to
marinate

COOK TIME:
1 hour
30 minutes

Dried fruits are often the key to sweet and savory Moroccan dishes. This dish is considered the ultimate one-pot dish. In Morocco, this tagine is served on top of a very soft, layered, freshly made bread called *rghifa* or *msemen*. This delicious bread is cut by hand to absorb all the goodness from this sweet and savory chicken dish, also called *trid*.

⅓ cup Karima's Chicken Spice Mix (page 178)

¼ preserved lemon, homemade (page 172) or store-bought, chopped, plus 1 tablespoon chopped

1 teaspoon kosher salt

½ teaspoon ras el hanout, homemade (page 15) or store-bought

¼ teaspoon saffron threads, crumbled

1 whole chicken (3 pounds), cut into 6 or 8 serving pieces

2 tablespoons extra-virgin olive oil, plus more for greasing the tagine

3 medium yellow onions, cut into ⅓-inch-thick slices

1 cinnamon stick

¼ cup water

¼ teaspoon smen or ghee or 1 tablespoon melted unsalted butter

1 cup loosely packed raisins

½ cup blanched almonds, toasted

1. In a large bowl, mix the spice mix, ¼ preserved lemon, the salt, ras el hanout, and saffron until it is a thick paste. Add the chicken, toss to coat, cover, and marinate for 15 minutes or up to overnight in the refrigerator.

2. Grease the inside of the tagine base with olive oil. Arrange half the onions in an even layer in the base and top with the chicken pieces from the center out, leaving 1½ inches around the edges. Arrange the remaining onions around the chicken and add the cinnamon stick.

3. Put the water, 2 tablespoons of olive oil, and the smen into the empty marinade bowl, swirl, and mix well. Pour it slowly all over the chicken and onions.

4. Cover the tagine, place it on a diffuser over low heat, and cook for 45 minutes. Check the liquid level and add boiling water as needed.

5. Uncover the tagine and scatter the raisins all over the chicken. Cover and continue cooking the tagine for 45 minutes, or until the chicken is cooked through (internal temperature of 165°F), the onions are caramelized, and the sauce is thick.

6. Set the tagine on a cooling rack to cool for 10 minutes. Serve garnished with the remaining 1 tablespoon of preserved lemon and the almonds.

COOKING TIP: Tagine with lots of onions can create a watery sauce, so be careful when adjusting the liquid level.

Roasted Chicken with Green Apples and Green Olives

SERVES 4

PREP TIME:
15 minutes,
plus
20 minutes
or up to
overnight to
marinate

COOK TIME:
1 hour
30 minutes

Beautiful and easy to make, this roast chicken dish does not need much attention. This sweet and savory tagine is an excellent family dinner and ideal for entertaining guests. If you'd like, you can add a drizzle of honey over the green apples to boost the flavor.

1 whole chicken (3 pounds), cut into 6 or 8 serving pieces

1 teaspoon kosher salt

⅓ cup Karima's Chicken Spice Mix (page 178)

¼ preserved lemon, homemade (page 172) or store-bought, chopped

½ teaspoon ras el hanout (page 15) or store-bought

¼ teaspoon saffron threads, crumbled, plus 3 or 4 threads

3 tablespoons extra-virgin olive oil, plus more for greasing the tagine

½ cup water

1 medium yellow onion, cut into ⅓-inch-thick slices

Boiling water

3 green apples, cored and cut into eighths

½ tablespoon freshly squeezed lemon juice

Pinch ground cinnamon

½ cup pitted green olives

1 tablespoon unsalted butter, melted

1. Place the chicken pieces on a baking sheet, rub them all over with salt, and set the pan aside.

2. In a food processor or using a mortar and pestle, combine the spice mix, preserved lemon, ras el hanout, and ¼ teaspoon of saffron to make a light spice paste.

3. Rub ¼ cup of the spice paste onto the chicken pieces and marinate them for 15 minutes or transfer the chicken to a bowl, cover, and marinate in the refrigerator overnight. Refrigerate the remaining spice mixture.

4. Position a rack in the center of the oven and preheat the oven to 375°F. Grease the inside of the tagine base with olive oil.

5. Arrange the onion slices across the base, then place the chicken pieces, skin-side up, on the onion. Add the water and 3 tablespoons of olive oil to the reserved spice paste and mix well. Pour the mixture all over the chicken and onion.

6. Place the uncovered tagine in the oven and roast for 1½ hours, or until the chicken is golden and the sauce is reduced by half. Check the liquid level and add boiling water as needed.

7. While the chicken is cooking, in a small bowl, toss together the apples, lemon juice, and cinnamon and set it aside. In another small bowl, mix ¼ cup of hot water with the melted butter and 3 or 4 saffron threads and set aside.

8. After 1½ hours of cooking, remove the tagine from the oven, arrange the apple slices around the chicken pieces, and scatter the olives over the top. Pour the melted butter mixture all over the apples and olives, return to the oven, and cook for 15 minutes, or until the apples are soft and the chicken has a crispy skin and reaches an internal temperature of 165°F. Remove the tagine from the oven, let it cool for 10 minutes, and enjoy!

COOKING TIP: Some green apples cook very fast and get mushy, so watch them carefully so they don't overcook. This dish is also lovely with pears.

Juicy Chicken Breast with Garlic Sauce, Mushrooms, and Onions

SERVES 4

PREP TIME:
15 minutes, plus 15 to 20 minutes to marinate

COOK TIME:
1 hour 30 minutes

Made with simple seasoned chicken breast in a light, flavorful tomato, mushroom, and garlic sauce, this is so easy to prepare! Slow-cooking these ingredients using a tagine coaxes maximum flavors from the aromatic herbs, garlic, spices, and preserved lemon. You can make this with many vegetable combinations; just use sturdier ones—like sweet potato, Brussels sprouts, and potatoes—because they cook in the same time as the chicken breast.

3 medium tomatoes, finely chopped, or 1½ cups canned crushed tomatoes

4 garlic cloves, peeled

3 tablespoons extra-virgin olive oil, divided, plus more for greasing the tagine

1¼ teaspoons kosher salt, divided

1 medium preserved lemon, homemade (page 172) or store-bought, finely chopped

⅓ cup Karima's Chicken Spice Mix (page 178)

¼ teaspoon cayenne pepper

¼ teaspoon finely chopped fresh rosemary

1½ pounds boneless, skinless chicken breast, cut into 3-inch pieces

1 large yellow onion, chopped

2 cups sliced cremini mushrooms

¼ cup water

Boiling water

1 tablespoon chopped scallion, chives, or parsley, for garnish

1. In a food processor, combine the tomatoes, garlic, 2 tablespoons of olive oil, and ¼ teaspoon of salt and pulse to combine. Set the tomato sauce aside.

2. In a large bowl, mix the remaining 1 teaspoon of salt, the preserved lemon, spice mix, cayenne, and rosemary until

it is a thick paste. Add the chicken, toss to coat, cover, and marinate in the refrigerator for 15 to 20 minutes.

3. Grease the inside of the tagine base with olive oil. Arrange the onion in an even layer in the base, top with the sliced mushrooms, and pour the tomato sauce over the vegetables. Add the chicken pieces from the center out.

4. Put the water into the empty marinade bowl and mix well. Pour it slowly all over the chicken, vegetables, and sauce and drizzle with the remaining 1 tablespoon of olive oil. Clean any splashes of sauce from the tagine sides.

5. Cover the tagine, place it on a diffuser over low heat, and cook for 1½ hours, or until the chicken is cooked through (internal temperature of 165ºF) and the sauce is reduced by half. Check the liquid level at 45 minutes and add boiling water as needed.

6. Set the tagine on a cooling rack to cool for 10 minutes. Serve garnished with chopped scallions.

VARIATION: Replace the mushrooms with green peas, sliced carrots, bell pepper, or sliced potato and add olives to the sauce.

Chicken Meatballs with Roasted Garlic, Onion, and Parsley

SERVES 4

PREP TIME:
25 minutes

COOK TIME:
1 hour
30 minutes

These well-seasoned chicken meatballs are incredibly flavorful, slow-cooked with the aroma of caramelized garlic and onions. The dish is packed with hearty, lemony, garlicky, and sweet flavors. The fragrance from each ingredient makes these meatballs so tasty by themselves tucked in a baguette or pita bread as a sandwich. Its complex flavors can be added to soups, sautéed vegetables, or served on the top of rice, pasta, quinoa, or Fluffy Couscous (page 170) for a complete family meal.

1 pound ground chicken breast

2 medium yellow onions, chopped, divided

⅓ cup Karima's Chicken Spice Mix (page 178)

2 tablespoons chopped fresh parsley, divided, plus more for garnish

1 teaspoon kosher salt, plus more for sprinkling

1 teaspoon grated lemon zest

½ teaspoon ground cumin

¼ teaspoon cayenne pepper

3 tablespoons extra-virgin olive oil, divided

4 garlic cloves, peeled

Boiling water

2 tablespoons freshly squeezed lemon juice

1. In a large bowl, mix the ground chicken, ½ cup of onion, the spice mix, 1 tablespoon of parsley, salt, lemon zest, cumin, and cayenne until well combined. If the mixture is a little dry, sprinkle in some water, then form it into 2-inch balls. The chicken meatballs can be made ahead and refrigerated in a covered container for up to 2 days.

2. Place 2 tablespoons of olive oil in the tagine base and set on a diffuser over medium-low heat. Heat the olive oil, then add the garlic. Use a wooden spatula to sauté the garlic until it is soft and lightly browned, about 3 minutes. Remove the garlic to a small bowl, then add the remaining chopped onions and sauté in the olive oil left in the tagine for 1 to 2 minutes.

3. Place the chicken balls on top of the onions and sauté for 10 minutes. Pour the ½ cup of hot or boiling water slowly around the edges of the tagine and cover the tagine. It is important to add hot water at a similar temperature as the tagine to avoid cracking it.

4. Use a spoon to smash the sautéed garlic, then add the lemon juice, remaining 1 tablespoon of olive oil, and remaining 1 tablespoon of parsley and mix well.

5. Uncover the tagine, evenly spread the garlic mixture over the chicken balls and onions, and sprinkle with salt. Cover the tagine and cook for 45 minutes, or until the chicken balls are cooked through (internal temperature of 165ºF) and the sauce is thick. Check the liquid level every 30 minutes and add boiling water as needed.

6. Set the tagine on a cooling rack to cool for 10 minutes. Serve garnished with parsley.

INGREDIENT TIP: If you want to make your own ground chicken, cut skinless breasts into small chunks and place them in a food processor. Pulse only 2 or 3 times, as you don't want to overgrind the meat.

Turkey Meatballs in Spicy Tomato Herb Sauce

SERVES 4

PREP TIME:
25 minutes

COOK TIME:
45 minutes

Here is a spin on a classic Moroccan dish, with turkey replacing the traditional beef. These meatballs are tender and flavored with onions, herbs, and spices cooked in a harissa-spiced tomato sauce. Use dark turkey meat here because it is fattier and will bring a deeper, richer flavor to the meatballs.

1 pound ground turkey

1½ medium yellow onions, finely chopped, divided

6 garlic cloves, minced, divided

4 tablespoons finely chopped fresh parsley, divided, plus more for garnish

⅓ cup Karima's Chicken Spice Mix (page 178)

1¼ teaspoons kosher salt, divided

1 teaspoon sweet paprika

½ teaspoon ground coriander

1 teaspoon harissa, homemade (page 174) or store-bought, divided

2 tablespoons extra-virgin olive oil, plus more for greasing the tagine

4 large tomatoes, finely chopped, or 2 (15-ounce) cans crushed tomatoes

½ teaspoon dried thyme or oregano

Boiling water

1. In a large bowl, mix the ground turkey, two-thirds of the chopped onion, half the garlic, 3 tablespoons of parsley, the spice mix, 1 teaspoon of salt, the paprika, coriander, and ½ teaspoon of harissa until well combined. Shape the turkey mixture into 2-inch meatballs and set them aside. If you have time, make the meatballs a few hours ahead so the meat can absorb all the flavors from the spices.

2. Grease the inside of the tagine base with a little olive oil. Add the tomatoes, 2 tablespoons of olive oil, the thyme, and remaining onions, the garlic, 1 tablespoon of parsley, ½ teaspoon of harissa, and ¼ teaspoon of salt and mix well. Place the meatballs in the sauce and wipe any sauce splashes off the edges of the tagine.

3. Cover the tagine, place it on a diffuser over medium-low heat, and cook for about 45 minutes, or until the meatballs are firm and cooked through (internal temperature of 165°F) and the tomato sauce is thick. Check the liquid level every 20 minutes and add boiling water as needed. While checking, use a spoon to pour some of the sauce over the meatballs.

4. Set the tagine on a cooling rack to cool for 7 minutes. Serve garnished with parsley.

INGREDIENT TIP: The best ground meat for tagines is at least 7 percent fat. If you don't use dark meat, always add a little fat to ground white meat (turkey or chicken) to help with moisture.

VARIATION: A variety of vegetables can be added to this dish, such as green peas, okra, or bell peppers, to make it a complete dinner.

Chicken and Chickpeas with Apricot and Ras el Hanout

SERVES 4

PREP TIME:
15 minutes, plus
10 minutes
or up to
overnight to
marinate

COOK TIME:
1 hour
40 minutes

Sweet and savory tagine dishes are most common in Moroccan cuisine. The key to the sweetness is fresh or dried fruits. In this recipe, the chicken is stewed with onion, chickpeas, and dried apricots in a fragrant sauce seasoned with ras el hanout—a vibrant, sweet, and warm spice mix. This dish is traditionally served with home-made bread, but it also goes well over Fluffy Couscous (page 170).

¼ cup Karima's Chicken Spice Mix (page 178)

3 tablespoons finely chopped preserved lemon, homemade (page 172) or store-bought, divided

1 teaspoon kosher salt

½ teaspoon ras el hanout, homemade (page 15) or store-bought

¼ teaspoon saffron threads, crumbled

1 whole chicken (3 pounds), cut into 6 serving pieces, or 2 pounds boneless, skinless chicken, cut into 6 pieces

2 tablespoons extra-virgin olive oil, plus more for greasing the tagine

1 medium yellow onion, chopped

1 (15-ounce) can chickpeas, drained and rinsed

½ cup water

1 cinnamon stick

Boiling water

1 cup dried apricots

1 tablespoon chopped fresh cilantro, for garnish

1. In a large bowl, mix the spice mix, 2 tablespoons of pre-served lemon, the salt, ras el hanout, and saffron. Add the chicken pieces, toss to coat, cover, and marinate for 10 minutes or up to overnight in the refrigerator.

2. Grease the inside of the tagine base with olive oil. Spread the onion in the base and layer the chickpeas on top of the onion. Place the marinated chicken pieces, working from the center out, on the top of the chickpeas and add the cinnamon stick to the edge.

3. Put ¼ cup of water and 2 tablespoons of olive oil into the empty marinade bowl, swirl, and pour the liquid all over the chicken, chickpeas, and onions. Pour the remaining ¼ cup of water around the edges of the tagine slowly.

4. Cover the tagine, place it on a diffuser over medium-low heat, and cook for 1 hour. Check the liquid level every 45 minutes and add boiling water as needed.

5. After 1 hour of cooking, uncover the tagine and distribute the apricots all over the top. Cover and cook for 40 minutes longer, or until the chicken is very tender, the onion and the chickpeas are soft, and the sauce is reduced but slightly thick.

6. Set the tagine on a cooling rack to cool for 10 minutes. Serve garnished with the remaining 1 tablespoon of preserved lemon and the cilantro.

COOKING TIP: If you are using dried chickpeas that you soak and cook at home, take care to add enough water because chickpeas are starchy, so they can thicken the sauce too much. This tip is not as crucial if using canned chickpeas.

Roasted Chicken Thighs with Preserved Lemon and Raisins

SERVES 4

PREP TIME:
15 minutes,
plus
10 minutes
or up to
overnight to
marinate

COOK TIME:
1 hour

These sour and sweet roasted chicken thighs are a delicious combination of tempting spices and tart citrus. It is a well-balanced dish, as the citrus is a bright counterpoint for the slightly fattier chicken thighs. This dish needs an earthy vegetable side dish or fresh salad to complement the richness.

¼ cup Karima's Chicken Spice Mix (page 178)

2 tablespoons finely chopped preserved lemon, homemade (page 172), or store-bought

1 teaspoon kosher salt

¼ teaspoon ground cardamom

8 medium boneless, skin-on chicken thighs

2 tablespoons extra-virgin olive oil, plus more for greasing the tagine

1 large yellow onion, cut into ⅓-inch-thick slices

½ cup water

4 slices (½-inch) orange

3 slices (½-inch) lemon

Boiling water

2 tablespoons unsalted butter, melted

¼ teaspoon grated orange zest

½ cup packed golden raisins, for garnish

1. In a large bowl, mix the spice mix, preserved lemon, salt, and cardamom. Add the chicken thighs, toss to coat, cover, and marinate for 10 minutes or up to overnight in the refrigerator.

2. Position a rack in the center of the oven and preheat the oven to 375ºF.

3. Grease the inside of the tagine base with olive oil. Lay the onion across the base, then place the marinated chicken thighs, skin-side up, on the onion.

4. Put ¼ cup of water and the olive oil into the empty marinade bowl, mix well, and pour the liquid over the chicken and onion. Pour another ¼ cup of water around the edges of the tagine and lay the orange and lemon slices around the chicken to create a pretty presentation.

5. Transfer the uncovered tagine to the oven and cook for 1 hour, or until the chicken thighs are cooked through (internal temperature of 165°F) and golden brown, the citrus slices and onion are caramelized, and the sauce is thick. Check the liquid level after 30 minutes and add boiling water as needed.

6. Meanwhile, in a small bowl, mix the melted butter and orange zest and set aside.

7. Remove the tagine from the oven and brush the melted butter mixture over the chicken thighs and top with the raisins.

8. Cover the tagine and set on a cooling rack to cool for 10 minutes before serving.

VARIATION: This dish would work with drumsticks as well. Check them after 45 minutes because this cut takes less time in the oven.

Duck with Caramelized Onions, Carrots, and Orange

SERVES 4

PREP TIME:
15 minutes,
plus
20 minutes
or up to
overnight to
marinate

COOK TIME:
1 hour
30 minutes

Orange and duck are a perfect combination of succulent meat and citrusy sauce that melts into the caramelized onions and carrots. If you're used to only cooking with chicken, you're in for a lovely experience. Duck is all dark meat–including the breast–and has a thick layer of fat underneath the skin. Balance the richness of this tagine with starchy grains or veggies, such as mashed potato, brown or white rice, or Fluffy Couscous (page 170).

½ cup Karima's Chicken Spice Mix (page 178)

1 tablespoon chopped preserved lemon, homemade (page 172) or store-bought

1 teaspoon kosher salt

¼ teaspoon ground cardamom

4 duck leg quarters

2 tablespoons extra-virgin olive oil, plus more for greasing the tagine

1 large yellow onion, cut into ⅓-inch-thick slices

½ cup water

¼ teaspoon grated orange zest

4 medium carrots, cut on the diagonal into 1-inch chunks

1 medium orange, halved and cut into ⅓-inch-thick slices

Boiling water

2 teaspoons toasted sesame seeds, for garnish

1. In a large bowl, mix the spice mix, preserved lemon, salt, and cardamom. Add the duck legs, toss to coat, cover, and marinate in the refrigerator for 20 minutes or up to overnight.

2. Preheat the oven to 375°F.

3. Grease the inside of the tagine base with olive oil. Lay the onion across the base, then place the marinated duck legs, skin-side up, in the center, crossing the bottom of the drumsticks over one another in the center.

4. Put ¼ cup of water, 2 tablespoons of olive oil, and the orange zest into the empty marinade bowl, mix well, and pour the liquid over the duck and onion. Pour another ¼ cup of water around the edges of the tagine. Lay the carrots around the duck, not covering it, and arrange the orange slices on the carrots.

5. Transfer the uncovered tagine to the oven and bake for 1½ hours, or until the duck is deep golden brown, the citrus slices and onion are caramelized, and the sauce is thickened. Check the liquid level after 45 minutes and add boiling water as needed.

6. Set the tagine on a cooling rack to cool for 10 minutes. Serve garnished with the sesame seeds.

COOKING TIP: The thick layer of fat over the duck meat means it takes longer to cook than chicken or turkey. But because it's dark meat, it won't dry out.

Roasted Chicken with Carrots and Green Peas

SERVES 4

PREP TIME:
15 minutes,
plus
15 minutes
or up to
overnight to
marinate

COOK TIME:
1 hour

Roasting chicken in a tagine is easy. Not only does roasting it in a tagine make it flavorful and delicious, it also requires less attention. This simple chicken and vegetable dish is a perfect example of traditional everyday Moroccan home cooking.

½ cup Karima's Chicken Spice Mix (page 178)

1 teaspoon kosher salt

¼ teaspoon ground cardamom

1 whole chicken (3 pounds), cut into 8 serving pieces

2 tablespoons extra-virgin olive oil, plus more for greasing the tagine

1 large yellow onion, cut into ⅓-inch-thick slices

3 cups fresh or frozen green peas

4 medium carrots, quartered

½ cup water

Boiling water

Preserved lemon, homemade (page 172) or store-bought, sliced, for garnish

1. In a large bowl, mix the spice mix, salt, and cardamom. Add the chicken pieces, toss to coat, cover, and marinate in the refrigerator for 20 minutes or up to overnight.

2. Position a rack in the bottom third of the oven and preheat the oven to 375°F.

3. Grease the inside of the tagine base with olive oil. Lay the onion across the base, then place the marinated chicken pieces, skin-side up, on top of the onion. Arrange the peas around the chicken and arrange the carrots on the peas.

4. Put ¼ cup of water and 2 tablespoons of olive oil into the empty marinade bowl, mix well, and pour the liquid over the chicken and vegetables. Pour another ¼ cup of water around the edges of the tagine.

5. Transfer the uncovered tagine to the oven and cook for 1 hour, or until the chicken is cooked through (internal temperature of 165ºF) and golden, the vegetables are tender, and the sauce is thickened. Check the liquid level after 30 minutes and add boiling water as needed.

6. Set the tagine on a cooling rack to cool for 10 minutes. Serve garnished with preserved lemon slices.

COOKING TIP: This is the ideal dish to play with because chicken combines well with most spices, herbs, and vegetables. For example, create a sweet dish by adding dried fruit. Or make it savory by adding sour olives. Or add both for a unique Moroccan flavor. Be creative!

Chicken with Green Beans

SERVES 4

PREP TIME:
15 minutes,
plus
15 minutes
or up to
overnight to
marinate

COOK TIME:
1 hour
30 minutes

Made with tender white and dark chicken meat pieces, this is a hearty, tasty stew. The flavor of the mild green beans is boosted with warm spices and preserved lemon. This dish goes well with other green vegetables in season, such as green peas, fava beans, cardoons, and artichokes.

½ cup Karima's Chicken Spice Mix (page 178)

2 tablespoons chopped preserved lemon, homemade (page 172) or store-bought

1 teaspoon kosher salt

½ teaspoon ras el hanout, homemade (page 15) or store-bought

1 whole chicken (3 pounds), cut into 8 serving pieces

2 tablespoons extra-virgin olive oil, plus more for greasing the tagine

1 large yellow onion, cut into ⅓-inch-thick slices

3 cups 3-inch pieces green beans, fresh or frozen

½ cup water

2 tablespoons chopped fresh cilantro, for garnish

1. In a large bowl, mix the spice mix, preserved lemon, salt, and ras el hanout. Add the chicken pieces, toss to coat, cover, and marinate for 15 minutes or up to overnight in the refrigerator.

2. Grease the inside of the tagine base with olive oil. Lay the onion across the base, then add the marinated chicken pieces, working from the center out, on top of the onion. Arrange the green beans around the chicken.

3. Put ¼ cup of water and 2 tablespoons of olive oil into the empty marinade bowl, mix well, and pour the liquid over the chicken and vegetables. Pour another ¼ cup of water around the edges of the tagine.

4. Cover the tagine, place it on a diffuser over medium-low heat, and cook for 1½ hours, or until the chicken is cooked through (internal temperature of 165°F), the vegetables are tender, and the sauce is reduced by half. Check the liquid level after 45 minutes and add boiling water as needed.

5. Set the tagine on a cooling rack to cool for 10 minutes. Serve garnished with cilantro.

INGREDIENT TIP: I don't recommend canned green beans for this dish because they are already soft and have lost their vibrant color. The best choice is fresh, in-season green beans, although flash-frozen green beans are the next best option.

Turkey Legs with Carrots, Preserved Lemon, and Green Olives

SERVES 4

PREP TIME:
15 minutes,
plus
15 minutes
or up to
overnight to
marinate

COOK TIME:
1 hour
30 minutes

Turkey is a wonderful alternative to chicken, and you can use the same spice mix used for chicken to create a flavorful tagine with sweet carrots and briny green olives. This is another easy dish to prepare, and the slow-cooking method makes the drumsticks so tender and juicy, you might never roast them again!

1 cup Karima's Chicken Spice Mix (page 178)

¼ preserved lemon, homemade (page 172) or store-bought, finely chopped

1 teaspoon kosher salt

¼ teaspoon ground cardamon

4 medium turkey drumsticks

2 tablespoons extra-virgin olive oil, plus more for greasing the tagine

1 large yellow onion, cut into ⅓-inch-thick slices

5 medium carrots, cut into 1-inch pieces

¾ cup water

Boiling water

1 cup pitted green olives

2 tablespoons chopped fresh cilantro, for garnish

1. In a large bowl, mix the spice mix, preserved lemon, salt, and cardamom to make a thin paste. Add the drumsticks, toss to coat, cover, and marinate for 15 minutes or up to overnight in the refrigerator.

2. Grease the inside of the tagine base with olive oil. Lay the onion across the base, then add the marinated turkey, from the center out, on top of the onion. Arrange the carrots around the turkey.

3. Put ¼ cup of water and 2 tablespoons of olive oil into the empty marinade bowl, mix well, and pour the liquid over the turkey and vegetables. Pour another ½ cup of water around the edges of the tagine.

4. Cover the tagine, place it on a diffuser over low heat, and cook for 1 hour. Check the liquid level after 45 minutes and add boiling water as needed.

5. Uncover the tagine, sprinkle the olives over everything, cover, and cook for 30 minutes longer, or until the turkey is cooked through (internal temperature of 165ºF), the vegetables are tender, and the sauce is creamy.

6. Set the tagine on a cooling rack to cool for 10 minutes. Serve garnished with cilantro.

Rolled Chicken Breast with Zucchini and Spinach

SERVES 4

PREP TIME:
15 minutes,
plus
20 minutes
or up to
overnight to
marinate

COOK TIME:
45 minutes

Chicken breasts are a staple in many homes because they are such an easy choice for fast meals. However, since they are naturally lean, they can be easily over-cooked, so the gentle tagine method is ideal. But to lift the everyday chicken breast out of the ordinary, try these marinated rolled chicken breasts. With gorgeous layers of zucchini and spinach, they are spectacular and definitely guest-worthy. Everyone will certainly think you worked over a stove all day.

½ cup Karima's Chicken Spice Mix (page 178)

1 teaspoon tomato paste

1 teaspoon kosher salt, plus more for sprinkling

½ teaspoon sweet paprika

8 thin-sliced chicken breast cutlets (4 ounces each)

2 medium zucchini, cut into ¼-inch-thick sticks

1½ cups baby spinach leaves

2 tablespoons extra-virgin olive oil, plus more for greasing the tagine

1 large yellow onion, cut into ⅓-inch-thick slices

½ cup water

Boiling water

½ cup chopped pitted Kalamata olives, for serving

1. In a large bowl, mix the spice mix, tomato paste, salt, and paprika to make a thin paste. Add the chicken, toss to coat, and marinate in the refrigerator for 20 minutes or up to overnight (the longer you can let it marinate, the more flavorful it will be).

2. When ready to cook, place the zucchini and spinach in a medium bowl, sprinkle with salt, and set aside.

3. Lay the chicken slices on a cutting board, top each with 1 slice of zucchini and a few spinach leaves, roll them up, and secure each with a toothpick.

4. Position a rack in the upper third of the oven and preheat the oven to 400°F.

5. Grease the inside of the tagine base with olive oil. Lay the onion across the base. Place the chicken rolls, seam-side down, on the vegetables, spaced a bit apart so they can cook evenly.

6. Put ¼ cup of water into the empty marinade bowl, mix well, and pour the liquid over the chicken and vegetables. Pour another ¼ cup of water around the edges of the tagine and drizzle the chicken rolls with 2 tablespoons of olive oil.

7. Transfer the uncovered tagine to the oven and cook for 45 minutes, or until the chicken is cooked through (internal temperature of 165°F) and slightly crispy, the vegetables are tender, and the sauce is reduced by half. Check the liquid level every 25 minutes and add boiling water as needed.

8. Set the tagine on a cooling rack to cool for 10 minutes. Serve topped with the olives.

INGREDIENT TIP: If you'd prefer, you can make your own chicken cutlets. Buy 4 chicken breasts and slice them horizontally in half.

Whole Roasted Stuffed Chicken

SERVES 4

PREP TIME:
15 minutes,
plus
20 minutes
or up to
overnight to
marinate

COOK TIME:
2 hours

Whole chicken stuffed with vegetables and olives, then slowly roasted to juicy perfection, is an exceptional meal to serve as a family dinner. Using an open tagine with the chicken set on a bed of onion allows the bird to roast slowly, creating a crispy, golden skin and succulent meat packed with amazing flavors. If you have the time, the whole chicken is best marinated for at least 2 hours (and ideally overnight), so it can absorb the garlic, preserved lemon, fresh ginger, and herb marinade.

¾ cup Karima's Chicken Spice Mix (page 178)

2 tablespoons finely chopped preserved lemon, homemade (page 172) or store-bought, plus slices for garnish

¼ teaspoon ground cardamom

1 whole chicken (3 pounds)

1¼ teaspoons kosher salt, divided

1 medium potato, cut into ½-inch cubes

1 medium carrot, cut into ½-inch cubes

½ cup cauliflower florets

½ cup green peas, fresh or frozen

¼ cup chopped pitted green or Kalamata olives

1 jalapeño pepper, seeded and chopped

2 tablespoons extra-virgin olive oil, divided, plus more for greasing the tagine

1 large yellow onion, cut into ⅓-inch-thick slices

½ cup water

Boiling water

Chopped fresh parsley, for garnish

1. In a large bowl, mix the spice mix, preserved lemon, and cardamom until combined.

2. Place the chicken on a sheet pan, sprinkle it inside and outside with 1 teaspoon of salt. Massage the chicken inside and outside with ½ cup of the spice paste and let it marinate in the refrigerator for 15 to 20 minutes or up to overnight.

3. In a medium bowl, combine the potato, carrot, cauliflower, peas, olives, and jalapeño. Add the remaining spice paste, ¼ teaspoon of salt, and 1 tablespoon of olive oil and toss to coat. Stuff the vegetables into the marinated chicken, secure the cavity with toothpicks, and set it aside.

4. Position a rack in the center of the oven and preheat the oven to 350ºF.

5. Grease the inside of the tagine base with olive oil. Lay the onion across the base and place the chicken, breast-side up, in the center.

6. Put ¼ cup water and the remaining 1 tablespoon of olive oil into the empty marinade bowl, swirl, and pour the liquid over the chicken and onion. Pour another ¼ cup of water around the edges of the tagine.

7. Transfer the uncovered tagine to the oven and roast for 2 hours, or until the chicken is cooked through (internal temperature of 165ºF) and golden, and the onion is caramelized into a thick sauce. Check on the liquid level every 45 minutes and add boiling water, 2 to 3 tablespoons at a time, as needed. Small amounts allow the ingredients to caramelize.

8. Set the tagine on a cooling rack to cool for 10 minutes. Remove the toothpicks and serve the tagine topped with sliced preserved lemon and parsley.

COOKING TIP: If you end up with a watery sauce, use a deep spoon to transfer the sauce to a small saucepan and cook it over medium heat until it reduces to the consistency of maple syrup. Then add the thickened sauce back to the tagine.

Chicken Drumsticks with Cabbage, Carrots, and Golden Raisins

PREP TIME:
15 minutes, plus
15 minutes or up to overnight to marinate

COOK TIME:
1 hour
30 minutes

Chicken drumsticks are a favorite meal choice worldwide. The combination of chicken drumsticks, winter veggies, and golden raisins makes this fragrant, sweet dish ideal for cooler months. Baking it in the oven creates a lovely golden skin on the drumsticks, but it can be cooked (covered) on the stovetop over medium-low heat for 1½ hours, or until the chicken reaches an internal temperature of 165ºF.

½ cup Karima's Chicken Spice Mix (page 178)

4 tablespoons chopped fresh cilantro, divided

3 tablespoons freshly squeezed lemon juice

2 tablespoons extra-virgin olive oil, plus more for greasing the tagine

1 teaspoon kosher salt

½ teaspoon sweet paprika

8 medium chicken drumsticks

5 garlic cloves, left whole

1 large yellow onion, cut into ⅓-inch-thick slices

3 cups chopped green cabbage

2 medium carrots, cut into thick sticks

½ cup water

Boiling water

¼ cup packed golden raisins

1. In large bowl, combine the spice mix, 2 tablespoons of cilantro, the lemon juice, olive oil, salt, and paprika to make a thin paste. Add the chicken drumsticks and whole garlic cloves, toss to coat, cover, and marinate for 15 minutes or up to overnight in the refrigerator.

2. Position a rack in the bottom third of the oven and preheat the oven to 375ºF.

3. Grease the inside of the tagine base with olive oil. Lay the onion across the base, then layer the cabbage, and then the carrots on top of the cabbage. Place the marinated chicken and garlic cloves on the vegetables, slightly apart, so the skin can crisp evenly—try to arrange the garlic around the edges.

4. Put ¼ cup of water into the empty marinade bowl, swirl, and pour the liquid over the chicken and vegetables. Pour another ¼ cup of water around the edges of the tagine.

5. Transfer the uncovered tagine to the oven and roast for 1½ hours, or until the chicken is cooked through (internal temperature of 165°F) and golden, the vegetables are caramelized, and the sauce is reduced by half. Check on the liquid level after 45 minutes and add boiling water as needed.

6. Set the tagine on a cooling rack, top with the raisins, cover, and let it cool for 10 minutes. Serve garnished with the remaining 2 tablespoons of cilantro.

INGREDIENT TIP: The cooking time can change depending on the size of the drumsticks. So try to buy similar pieces and always check on the drumsticks while cooking to ensure they don't overcook.

SEAFOOD

◀ **Seafood Paella with Chermoula, 126**

Mussels in Spicy Tomato Herb Sauce

SERVES 4

PREP TIME:
15 minutes,
plus
20 minutes
or up to
overnight to
marinate

COOK TIME:
1 hour

In Morocco, most towns and cities on the coast consume lots of seafood, and this mussel tagine is very popular. The herb tomato sauce with chermoula is the perfect creation for cooking the mussels. This dish is easy to prepare and quick, especially when the chermoula mixture is premade.

1½ pounds frozen cooked mussel meat, thawed

4 tablespoons chermoula, homemade (page 175) or store-bought, divided

3 tablespoons extra-virgin olive oil

4 large tomatoes, finely chopped, or 2 (15-ounce) cans crushed tomatoes

1 tablespoon tomato paste

1 tablespoon chopped fresh cilantro

1 tablespoon dried thyme

2 teaspoons harissa, homemade (page 174) or store-bought

¼ teaspoon kosher salt

Boiling water

1 tablespoon chopped fresh parsley, for garnish

1. In a large bowl, toss the mussel meat with 3 tablespoons of chermoula, cover, and marinate in the refrigerator for 20 minutes or up to overnight.

2. Grease the tagine base with 3 tablespoons of olive oil and make sure the sides are covered. Add the tomatoes, tomato paste, cilantro, thyme, harissa, salt, and remaining 1 tablespoon of chermoula to the tagine. Mix the ingredients together.

3. Cover the tagine, place it on a diffuser over medium-low heat, and cook for 40 minutes, or until the sauce is creamy. Check the liquid level every 20 minutes and add boiling water by the tablespoon, as needed.

4. Add the marinated mussels, cover, and cook for 20 minutes to heat through and allow the flavors to meld.

5. Set the tagine on a cooling rack to cool for 7 minutes. Serve garnished with the parsley.

SERVING TIP: Serve this with a salad and crusty baguette or rustic bread to soak up all the flavorful sauce.

Stuffed Calamari in Harissa Sauce

SERVES 4

PREP TIME:
20 minutes, plus
20 minutes
or up to
overnight to
marinate

COOK TIME:
1 hour

Moroccan cuisine is rich in seafood dishes because of its long coastline, and the dishes are prepared in a variety of ways depending on the region. This stuffed calamari in spicy tomato sauce might seem complicated, but is incredibly easy to make. The filling can be any leftover rice, quinoa, or shredded vegetables you have on hand. Serve this dish over quinoa, pasta, or with rustic bread so you can scoop up every bit of the delectable sauce.

4 calamari, cleaned

5 tablespoons chermoula, homemade (page 175) or store-bought, divided

2 cups rice vermicelli

Boiling water

½ cup chopped bell peppers (any color)

½ cup chopped pitted green olives

3 tablespoons extra-virgin olive oil, divided, plus more for greasing the tagine

¼ teaspoon kosher salt

4 large tomatoes, chopped, or 4 cups canned crushed tomatoes

2 tablespoons chopped fresh cilantro, divided

1 tablespoon chopped fresh parsley

1 tablespoon tomato paste

2 teaspoons harissa, homemade (page 174) or store-bought

1. In a large bowl, toss the calamari with 2 tablespoons of chermoula, coating it inside and out. Cover and marinate in the refrigerator for 20 minutes or up to overnight.

2. Place the rice vermicelli in a medium bowl, add 2 cups of boiling water, and soak it for 2 minutes. Drain the noodles and cut them into ⅛-inch pieces while still hot. Return them to the bowl and add the bell peppers, olives, 2 tablespoons of chermoula, 1 tablespoon of olive oil, and the salt and toss to mix.

3. Place the marinated calamari on a cutting board and stuff each calamari with the rice vermicelli mixture. Secure each one closed with toothpicks.

4. Grease the inside of the tagine base with olive oil. Add the tomatoes, 1 tablespoon of cilantro, the parsley, tomato paste, harissa, remaining 2 tablespoons of olive oil, and remaining 1 tablespoon of chermoula and stir to combine. Arrange the stuffed calamari in the tomato mixture.

5. Cover the tagine, place it on a diffuser over medium-low heat, and cook for 1 hour, or until the calamari are tender and the sauce is creamy. Check the liquid level every 20 minutes and add boiling water by the tablespoon, as needed.

6. Set the tagine on a cooling rack to cool for 7 minutes. Serve garnished with the remaining 1 tablespoon of cilantro.

Shrimp with Roasted Pepper, Tomato, and Chermoula

SERVES 4

PREP TIME:
45 minutes, plus
20 minutes or up to overnight to marinate

COOK TIME:
50 minutes

Roasted red peppers, fresh tomatoes, and chermoula form the delightful base for this flavorful shrimp tagine. This dish is wonderful for lunch or dinner, especially if accompanied by vegetarian side dishes, fresh green salad, and crusty bread. You can also serve it as an appetizer.

1½ pounds large shrimp (31/35 count), peeled, deveined, and tails removed

3 tablespoons chermoula, homemade (page 175) or store-bought, divided

3 tablespoons extra-virgin olive oil, plus more for greasing the tagine

2 large tomatoes, chopped, or 2 cups canned diced tomatoes

2 medium roasted bell peppers (green or red), chopped

1 medium red onion, chopped

1 tablespoon tomato paste

2 tablespoons chopped fresh cilantro, divided

Pinch kosher salt

1 lemon, cut into 8 wedges

Boiling water

1. In a large bowl, toss the shrimp with 2 tablespoons of chermoula, cover, and marinate in the refrigerator for 20 minutes.

2. Grease the inside of the tagine base with olive oil. Add the tomatoes, roasted peppers, onion, 3 tablespoons of olive oil, the tomato paste, remaining 1 tablespoon of chermoula, 1 tablespoon of cilantro, and salt and stir to combine.

3. Cover the tagine, place it on a diffuser set over medium-low heat, and cook for 30 minutes, or until the sauce is thick.

4. After 30 minutes, uncover the tagine, arrange the marinated shrimp and 4 of the lemon wedges in a nice presentation, cover, and cook for 15 to 20 minutes, until the shrimp are pink and opaque and the sauce is creamy. Check the liquid level every 15 minutes and add boiling water by the tablespoon, as needed.

5. Set the tagine on a cooling rack to cool for 7 minutes. Serve garnished with the remaining 1 tablespoon of cilantro and the lemon wedges.

MAKE AHEAD: All the prep for this dish can be done the day before, so you can jump right into cooking the next day. The roasted pepper and tomato sauce can be cooked completely, transferred to a jar or container, topped with a couple of tablespoons of olive oil, and refrigerated for up to 4 days.

Shrimp and Mushrooms in Tomato Oregano Sauce

SERVES 4

PREP TIME:
45 minutes,
plus
20 minutes
or up to
overnight to
marinate

COOK TIME:
55 minutes

Shrimp dishes are a lifesaver when you are pressed for a quick meal, and this is quite possibly the easiest tagine because shrimp and mushroom cook in no time at all. The combination of garlic, citrusy chermoula, and sweet shrimp with the earthy flavor of mushroom in a sweet and spicy oregano tomato sauce is a well-balanced, flavorful meal.

1½ pounds large shrimp (³¹⁄₃₅ count), peeled and deveined

3 tablespoons chermoula, homemade (page 175) or store-bought, divided

3 tablespoons extra-virgin olive oil, divided

3 cups chopped cremini mushrooms

½ medium red onion, finely chopped

2 large tomatoes, chopped, or 2 cups canned diced tomatoes

½ teaspoon chopped fresh oregano

Pinch kosher salt

Boiling water

1 tablespoon chopped fresh parsley, for garnish

4 lemon wedges

1. In a large bowl, toss the shrimp and 2 tablespoons of chermoula, cover, and marinate in the refrigerator for 20 minutes.

2. Place 2 tablespoons of olive oil in the tagine base and set on a diffuser over medium-low heat. Add the mushrooms and onion and sauté for about 7 minutes, or until the vegetables are softened.

3. Add the tomatoes, remaining 1 tablespoon of chermoula, remaining 1 tablespoon of olive oil, the oregano, and salt. Cover and cook for 25 minutes, or until the sauce is thick.

4. After 25 minutes, uncover the tagine, arrange the marinated shrimp in a nice presentation, cover, and cook for 15 to 20 minutes, until the shrimp are pink and opaque and the sauce is creamy. Check the liquid level every 15 minutes, and add boiling water by the tablespoon, as needed.

5. Set the tagine on a cooling rack to cool for 7 minutes. Serve garnished with parsley and lemon wedges for squeezing.

COOKING TIP: The best—and safest—way to thaw frozen shrimp is in a colander set over a bowl in the refrigerator overnight.

Tuna with Chermoula in Roasted Garlic Cumin Sauce

PREP TIME:
15 minutes,
plus 20 to
30 minutes
to marinate

COOK TIME:
35 minutes

Tuna is a firm-fleshed fish that cooks well in a tagine as steaks, kebabs, or cubes because it does not fall apart while cooking. But it can be overcooked, so watch carefully. In this dish, chermoula gives the tuna a flavorful boost and keeps it moist.

1½ pounds tuna steak, cut into 2-inch cubes

2 tablespoons chermoula, homemade (page 175) or store-bought

2 tablespoons extra-virgin olive oil

3 cups halved cherry or grape tomatoes

2 jalapeño peppers, seeded and thinly sliced

1 cup chopped scallions, white and green parts

4 Roasted Garlic (page 173) cloves

½ cup hot water

2 tablespoons salted butter, melted

2 tablespoons freshly squeezed lemon juice

½ teaspoon ground cumin

¼ teaspoon kosher salt

Boiling water

1 tablespoon chopped fresh cilantro, for garnish

1. In a large bowl, toss the tuna and chermoula, cover, and marinate in the refrigerator for 20 to 30 minutes.

2. Add the olive oil to the tagine base and set it on a diffuser over medium-low heat. Heat the oil for 2 minutes.

3. Pull the tuna pieces from the marinade (reserving the marinade) and add them to the tagine. Sauté for about 1½ minutes, or until firm on both sides and still slightly moist in the center. Transfer the tuna to a large plate.

4. Add the cherry tomatoes, jalapeños, scallions, and roasted garlic to the tagine. Return the tuna to the tagine. Put the hot water, melted butter, lemon juice, cumin, and salt into the empty marinade bowl, stirring to combine. Pour the mixture over the tuna and vegetables in the tagine.

5. Cover the tagine and cook for 20 to 30 minutes, or until the tuna is cooked but the center is still moist, the cherry tomatoes are soft, and the sauce is creamy. Check the liquid level every 20 minutes and add boiling water by the tablespoon, as needed.

6. Set the tagine on a cooling rack to cool for 4 to 5 minutes. Serve garnished with the cilantro.

COOKING TIP: When cooked, tuna should be still be moist in the very center because once it is overcooked, there is no going back.

Salmon with Layered Vegetables and Preserved Lemon

SERVES 4

PREP TIME:
15 minutes,
plus
20 minutes
or up to
overnight to
marinate

COOK TIME:
1 hour

An extremely popular tagine dish in Morocco, this is commonly made with white-fleshed fish, but salmon is a great match for the sharp flavors here: preserved lemon, chermoula, and jalapeño. The vegetables must be thinly sliced so they will cook in the same time it takes the salmon to be cooked through.

4 skinless salmon fillets (5 ounces each)

3 tablespoons chermoula, homemade (page 175) or store-bought

3 tablespoons extra-virgin olive oil, plus more for greasing the tagine

4 medium carrots, cut on the diagonal into ⅛-inch-thick slices

3 medium potatoes, thinly sliced

2 medium bell peppers (any color), cut crosswise into ⅛-inch-thick rings

2 medium tomatoes, cut into ¼-inch-thick slices

1 small lemon, sliced

1 or 2 jalapeño peppers, halved and seeded

½ cup hot water

2 tablespoons chopped fresh cilantro, divided

¼ teaspoon kosher salt

Boiling water

1. In a large bowl, toss the salmon and chermoula, cover, and marinate in the refrigerator for 20 minutes or up to overnight.

2. Grease the inside of the tagine base with olive oil and lay the carrots across the base. Then add the potato slices, bell peppers, tomatoes, and lemon slices to create a beautiful presentation when serving. Arrange the salmon pieces and jalapeños on top of the lemon slices.

3. Put ½ cup of hot water, 3 tablespoons of olive oil, 1 tablespoon of cilantro, and the salt into the empty marinade bowl, stirring to combine. Pour the mixture over the salmon and vegetables in the tagine.

4. Cover the tagine, place it on a diffuser over medium-low heat, and cook for 1 hour, or until the salmon is firm and flaky, the vegetables are tender, and the sauce is smooth. Check the liquid level every 20 minutes and add boiling water by the tablespoon, as needed.

5. Set the tagine on a cooling rack to cool for 7 minutes. Serve garnished with the remaining 1 tablespoon of cilantro.

VARIATION: If you'd prefer, use 1 tablespoon of harissa in place of the fresh jalapeños called for. Add it to the marinade bowl along with the hot water.

Spicy Baked Fish in Harissa Tomato Sauce with Olives

SERVES 4

PREP TIME:
20 minutes,
plus
30 minutes
or up to
overnight to
marinate

COOK TIME:
40 minutes

Easy to make in the oven, this classic Moroccan fish tagine is a whole marinated fish baked in an herbed, zesty tomato harissa sauce studded with olives.

½ cup freshly squeezed lemon juice

2 tablespoons extra-virgin olive oil, divided, plus more for greasing the tagine

4 garlic cloves, minced

1 tablespoon chopped fresh sage

2 teaspoons harissa, homemade (page 174) or store-bought, divided

2 teaspoons grated lemon zest

1 whole white fish (2 pounds), cleaned and scaled

1 teaspoon kosher salt, plus a pinch

1 large yellow onion, cut into ⅓-inch-thick slices

2 large tomatoes, finely chopped, or 2 cups canned diced tomatoes

½ teaspoon freshly ground black pepper

1 small lemon, cut into 7 wedges, divided

¼ cup hot water

Boiling water

1 tablespoon chopped fresh cilantro, for garnish

1. In a small bowl, combine the lemon juice, 1 tablespoon of olive oil, the garlic, sage, 1 teaspoon of harissa, and the lemon zest.

2. Place the whole fish on a baking sheet and make three diagonal cuts on each side of the thickest part of the fish. Rub the fish inside and outside with the salt, then rub it with 2 tablespoons of the lemon mixture. Cover the fish with plastic wrap and marinate it in the refrigerator for 30 minutes or up to overnight.

3. Preheat the oven to 400°F.

4. Grease the inside of the tagine base with olive oil. Lay the onion slices across the base and spread the tomatoes over the onion. Sprinkle the pepper over the vegetables. Place 3 lemon wedges in the fish cavity and lay the fish on the vegetables.

5. Put the hot water, remaining 1 tablespoon of olive oil, remaining 1 teaspoon of harissa, and a pinch of salt into the empty marinade bowl, swirl, and pour it gently around the onion and tomatoes, so the marinade stays on the fish.

6. Transfer the uncovered tagine to the oven and cook for 40 minutes, or until the tomatoes and onion are caramelized, the fish is slightly golden and firm, and the sauce is creamy. Check the liquid level every 20 minutes and add boiling water by the tablespoon, as needed.

7. Set the tagine on a cooling rack to cool for 10 minutes. Serve garnished with cilantro and the remaining lemon wedges.

COOKING TIP: Fish tagines can be cooked beautifully on the stovetop; just substitute the whole fish with any firm fish fillets.

Lemon Herbed Tuna Steak with Garlic Butter Potatoes

SERVES 4

PREP TIME:
15 minutes, plus 1 hour or up to overnight to marinate

COOK TIME:
40 minutes

Tuna tagine with potato is one of my favorites, with its garlicky, buttery, salty, and savory flavor. The tuna steak is lovely and meaty, and the potatoes add a satisfying thickness to the sauce. If you can't find tuna, any firm white fish will also work in this easy recipe.

¼ cup freshly squeezed lemon juice

5 garlic cloves, minced, divided

2 teaspoons harissa, homemade (page 174) or store-bought

1½ teaspoons chopped fresh rosemary, divided

1¼ teaspoons ground cumin, divided

1 teaspoon kosher salt, plus more for sprinkling

4 tuna steaks (4 ounces each)

2 tablespoons extra-virgin olive oil, plus more for greasing the tagine

2 celery stalks, cut into 2-inch pieces

2 large potatoes, cut into ⅛-inch-thick slices

½ cup hot water

Boiling water

4 tablespoons (½ stick) salted butter, melted

1 tablespoon chopped fresh cilantro, for garnish

1. In a large bowl, combine the lemon juice, 3 minced garlic cloves, the harissa, 1 teaspoon of rosemary, 1 teaspoon of cumin, and 1 teaspoon of salt. Add the tuna steaks, turn to coat, cover, and marinate in the refrigerator for 1 hour or up to overnight.

2. Preheat the oven to 400°F.

3. Grease the inside of the tagine base with olive oil. Lay the celery pieces across the base, then arrange the potato slices in concentric circles over the celery. Sprinkle the potatoes with some salt and the remaining ½ teaspoon of rosemary and place the tuna steaks on the potatoes.

4. Put ½ cup of hot water and 2 tablespoons of olive oil into the empty marinade bowl, swirl, and pour it over the tuna and vegetables.

5. Transfer the uncovered tagine to the oven and cook for 30 to 40 minutes, until the fish is firm, the potatoes are soft, and the sauce is creamy. Check the liquid level every 20 minutes and add boiling water by the tablespoon, as needed. In the last 10 minutes of cooking, in a small bowl, mix the melted butter, remaining 2 minced garlic cloves, and remaining ¼ teaspoon of cumin and spoon the mixture over the tuna and potatoes.

6. Set the tagine on a cooling rack to cool for 10 minutes. Serve garnished with the cilantro.

VARIATION: The marinade used in this recipe is perfect if you want to make tuna kebabs instead and grill them for 5 to 6 minutes.

Red Snapper with Roasted Garlic and Fresh Lemon

SERVES 4

PREP TIME:
15 minutes,
plus
15 minutes
or up to
overnight to
marinate

COOK TIME:
30 minutes

Sweet, lemony, and garlicky, this fish tagine is delicious with the hints of sweetness from the fennel and a drizzle of honey at the end, but you can shift the balance and increase the spice level if you'd like. Red snapper is a moist and delicate fish, and its mild taste goes well with any kind of additional flavors. So, experiment with different vegetables, spices, and herbs.

¼ cup freshly squeezed lemon juice

3 tablespoons salted butter, melted

2 tablespoons extra-virgin olive oil, plus more for greasing the tagine

4 garlic cloves, minced

1 teaspoon kosher salt, plus more as desired

¼ teaspoon grated peeled fresh ginger or 1 teaspoon ground ginger

¼ teaspoon ground fennel, plus fennel seeds for garnish

4 red snapper fillets (5 ounces each)

3 fennel bulbs, thinly sliced

Boiling water

½ medium lemon, thinly sliced

¼ teaspoon red pepper flakes, for garnish

Honey, for garnish

1. In a large bowl, combine the lemon juice, melted butter, 2 tablespoons of olive oil, the garlic, salt, ginger, and ground fennel. Add the fish, turn to coat, cover, and marinate for 15 minutes or up to overnight in the refrigerator.

2. Preheat the oven to 400°F.

3. Grease the inside of the tagine base with olive oil. Lay the fennel slices across the base and arrange the marinated fish on the fennel.

4. Put 2 tablespoons of boiling water into the empty marinade bowl, swirl, and pour it gently over the fish and fennel. Arrange the lemon slices around the fish.

5. Transfer the uncovered tagine to the oven and cook for 30 minutes, or until the fish flakes easily with a fork and the fennel is tender. Check the liquid level every 15 minutes and add boiling water by the tablespoon, as needed.

6. Set the tagine on a cooling rack to cool for 10 minutes. Serve garnished with fennel seeds, red pepper flakes, and a drizzle of honey.

Salmon with Roasted Garlic over Herbed Red Potatoes

SERVES 4

PREP TIME:
15 minutes, plus 1 hour or up to overnight to marinate

COOK TIME:
40 minutes

The two main ingredients in this tagine—salmon and potatoes—can be swapped out for any fish or vegetable you have in the refrigerator or what is on sale. These kinds of dishes allow your creativity to shine. (See a couple of suggestions for how to change it up in the Variations on page 117.)

2 tablespoons freshly squeezed lemon juice

2 tablespoons water

3 garlic cloves, minced

1½ teaspoons minced fresh thyme, divided

1 teaspoon kosher salt, divided

¾ teaspoon freshly ground black pepper, divided

4 skinless salmon fillets (4 ounces each)

2 tablespoons extra-virgin olive oil, divided, plus more for greasing the tagine

1 medium yellow onion, cut into ⅓-inch-thick slices

1 pound small red potatoes, halved

½ cup hot water

4 Roasted Garlic (page 173) cloves

4 tablespoons (½ stick) unsalted butter, melted

4 sprigs fresh thyme, for garnish

1. In a large bowl, combine the lemon juice, water, garlic, 1 teaspoon of thyme, ½ teaspoon of salt, and ½ teaspoon of pepper to form a thin paste. Add the salmon and turn to coat. Cover and marinate in the refrigerator for 1 hour or up to overnight.

2. Grease the inside of the tagine base with olive oil. Lay the onion across the base, then the potato halves. Sprinkle with the remaining ½ teaspoon of thyme, ½ teaspoon

of salt, and ¼ teaspoon of pepper, and drizzle with 1 tablespoon of olive oil. Pour ½ cup of hot water around the edges of the tagine base.

3. Cover the tagine, place it on a diffuser over medium-low heat, and cook for 30 minutes.

4. Uncover the tagine and arrange the roasted garlic and salmon on the softened potatoes. Put the melted butter and remaining 1 tablespoon of olive oil into the empty marinade bowl, swirl, and pour the mixture over the salmon and vegetables in the tagine.

5. Cover the tagine and cook for about 10 minutes, or until the salmon is firm and flakes when pressed with a fork and the potatoes are soft.

6. Set the tagine on a cooling rack to cool for 7 minutes. Serve garnished with thyme sprigs.

VARIATIONS: This simple recipe can be elevated for entertaining or a special occasion by adding sautéed mushrooms to the potatoes and ¼ cup of half-and-half to the butter mixture. Or try it with a spicy tomato sauce, like the one in Stuffed Calamari in Harissa Sauce (page 100).

Crab Meatballs and Green Peas in Tomato Habanero Sauce

PREP TIME:
20 minutes

COOK TIME:
45 minutes

Like other meatballs prepared in a tagine, this classic crab meatball dish is easy to make. The tender meatballs are cooked in a spicy tomato habanero sauce that gets an earthy, sweet flavor from green peas.

½ pound fresh, frozen, or canned crabmeat

1 cup cooked sweet (sticky) rice or 1 cup fine dried bread crumbs

2 large eggs, beaten

3 tablespoons chermoula, homemade (page 175) or store-bought, divided

2 tablespoons chopped fresh cilantro, divided

¼ teaspoon kosher salt

2 tablespoons extra-virgin olive oil, plus more for greasing the tagine

5 large tomatoes, chopped, or 5 cups canned crushed tomatoes

1 cup frozen green peas

1 tablespoon chopped fresh parsley, plus more for garnish

3 garlic cloves, minced

1 teaspoon habanero sauce or other hot pepper sauce

Boiling water

1. In a large bowl, combine the crab, rice, eggs, 2 tablespoons of chermoula, 1 tablespoon of cilantro, and the salt until well mixed. The mixture should hold together when pressed. If it's too wet, add more rice; if it's too dry, add water by the tablespoon. Form the mixture into meatballs about 1½ inches in diameter. Arrange on a plate, cover, and refrigerate.

2. Grease the inside of the tagine base with olive oil. Add the tomatoes, peas, parsley, garlic, remaining 1 tablespoon of chermoula, remaining 1 tablespoon of cilantro, 2 tablespoons of olive oil, and the habanero sauce, stirring to combine.

3. Cover the tagine, place it on a diffuser over medium-low heat, and cook for 15 minutes.

4. Uncover the tagine and arrange the meatballs in the tomato sauce. Cover the tagine and cook for 25 to 30 minutes, until the meatballs are firm and the sauce is thickened. Check the liquid level every 15 minutes and add boiling water by the tablespoon, as needed.

5. Set the tagine on a cooling rack to cool for 5 minutes. Serve garnished with parsley.

INGREDIENT TIP: If using imitation crabmeat, marinate it with chermoula for 10 minutes before adding it to the mixture. Sticky rice works especially well with this dish, but you can use any leftover rice.

Cod with Saffron, Raisins, and Caramelized Onions

SERVES 4

PREP TIME:
15 minutes, plus
30 minutes or up to overnight to marinate

COOK TIME:
45 minutes

Sweet cod tagine is a unique dish that combines an earthy mix of spices, golden raisins, and caramelized onions. The golden raisins are the perfect enhancement to bring an amazing finish to the dish, especially when combined with fragrant ras el hanout. You can replace the raisins with any dried fruit, such as dried apricots or dates, but don't omit them completely because they bring a natural sweetness to the fish.

3 garlic cloves, minced

1¼ teaspoons ras el hanout, homemade (page 15) or store-bought

1 teaspoon kosher salt

½ teaspoon grated lemon zest

¼ teaspoon saffron threads, crumbled

5 tablespoons water

4 cod fillets (5 ounces each)

3 tablespoons extra-virgin olive oil, divided, plus more for greasing the tagine

2 medium yellow onions, 1 cut into ⅓-inch-thick slices, 1 cut into thin half-moons

¼ cup water

Boiling water

1 cup loosely packed golden raisins

Pinch ground cinnamon

1 tablespoon toasted sesame seeds, for garnish

1. In a small bowl, combine the garlic, ras el hanout, salt, lemon zest, saffron, and water to form a thin paste.

2. In a large bowl, combine the cod and 3 tablespoons of the spice paste, toss to coat, cover, and marinate in the refrigerator for 30 minutes or up to overnight. Cover the remaining spice paste and set it aside.

3. Grease the inside of the tagine base with olive oil. Lay the thick onion slices across the base, then the thin onion half-moons. Stir ¼ cup of water and 2 tablespoons of olive oil into the reserved spice paste and spoon it over the onions.

4. Cover the tagine, place it on a diffuser over medium-low heat, and cook for 30 minutes, or until the onions are lightly caramelized.

5. Uncover the tagine and arrange the cod on the onions. Put ¼ cup of hot or boiling water into the empty marinade bowl, swirl, and pour the mixture over the fish and onions. Drizzle with the remaining 1 tablespoon of olive oil, spread the raisins in the tagine, and sprinkle with the cinnamon.

6. Cover the tagine and cook for about 25 minutes, or until the cod flakes when pressed with a fork, the onions are caramelized, and the sauce is creamy.

7. Set the tagine on a cooling rack to cool for 5 minutes. Serve garnished with sesame seeds.

SERVING TIP: This sweet fish tagine can be served over fluffy, buttery couscous, saffron basmati rice, or quinoa.

Spicy Calamari, Baby Octopus, and Mussels in Tomato Harissa Sauce

SERVES 4

PREP TIME:
15 minutes,
plus
30 minutes
or up to
overnight to
marinate

COOK TIME:
50 minutes

Seafood tagine is popular throughout Morocco for its simplicity and comforting, satisfying flavors. This dish is easy to make and cooking it in a tagine is a breeze. The calamari meat and octopus can be deliciously tender when prepared carefully.

1 (2-pound) package frozen mixed seafood (calamari, octopus, mussels), thawed

3 tablespoons chermoula, homemade (page 175) or store-bought, divided

3 tablespoons extra-virgin olive oil

½ medium red onion, chopped

5 large tomatoes, chopped, or 5 cups canned crushed tomatoes

1 tablespoon tomato paste

½ tablespoon chopped fresh cilantro

1 teaspoon harissa, homemade (page 174) or store-bought

½ teaspoon dried oregano

Pinch kosher salt

Boiling water

1 tablespoon chopped fresh parsley, for garnish

1. In a large bowl, toss the mixed seafood with 2 tablespoons of chermoula, cover, and marinate in the refrigerator for 30 minutes or up to overnight.

2. Place 2 tablespoons of olive oil in the tagine base and set on a diffuser over medium-low heat. Heat the oil for 2 minutes. then add the onion and sauté for 2 minutes. Add the marinated seafood pieces and cook for 4 minutes.

3. Add the tomatoes by tablespoons (so the tagine does not crack), then add the remaining 1 tablespoon of chermoula, remaining 1 tablespoon of olive oil, the tomato paste, cilantro, harissa, oregano, and salt, stirring to combine.

4. Cover the tagine and cook for 45 minutes, or until the seafood is tender and the sauce is thick. Check the liquid level every 20 minutes and add boiling water by the tablespoon, as needed.

5. Set the tagine on a cooling rack to cool for 5 minutes. Serve garnished with parsley.

COOKING TIP: It is best to thaw the seafood mix by rinsing it in cold water, setting it in a colander set inside a bowl, and leaving it in the refrigerator overnight or at least 3 hours before cooking.

Rockfish Fillets in Herb-Infused Oil with Lemon and Roasted Garlic

PREP TIME:
15 minutes

COOK TIME:
20 minutes

This delicious tagine is made in the oven, so make sure you watch it closely to avoid overcooking the fish. Try adding asparagus, cherry tomatoes, or thinly sliced mushrooms to the tagine for a delicious variation.

4 rockfish fillets
(5 ounces each)

1 teaspoon kosher salt

¾ teaspoon ground cumin

2 tablespoons extra-virgin
olive oil

1 tablespoon Herb-Infused
Olive Oil (page 176), preferably
made with thyme

2 tablespoons salted
butter, melted

4 garlic cloves, sliced

¼ cup freshly squeezed
lemon juice

1 lemon, cut into thin slices

¼ teaspoon red pepper flakes

1 tablespoon chopped fresh
cilantro, for garnish

1. Preheat the oven to 400°F.

2. Rub the fish with the salt and cumin on both sides and set them aside.

3. Place 2 tablespoons of olive oil, the herb-infused oil, melted butter, and roasted garlic in the tagine base and set on a diffuser over medium-low heat. Let it heat for 1 minute, then add the lemon juice.

4. Use a spoon to lay 5 lemon slices in the tagine base, then arrange the fish on the top of lemon slices. Spoon the sauce over the fish, place the remaining lemon slices on the fillets, and sprinkle them with the red pepper flakes.

5. Carefully transfer the uncovered tagine to the oven and cook for 15 minutes, or until the fish fillets are firm and flaky yet still moist. (If the fish fillets are thick, the safe internal temperature should reach 145°F.)

6. Set the tagine on a cooling rack, cover it, and let it cool for 8 to 10 minutes. Serve garnished with the cilantro.

SERVING TIP: You will want to serve the fish with a starchy staple, such as Fluffy Couscous (page 170), rice, or quinoa, to absorb all the lovely butter and herbed oil.

Seafood Paella with Chermoula

SERVES 4

PREP TIME:
45 minutes,
plus
35 minutes
to soak the
rice and
marinate

COOK TIME:
1 hour

An ancient dish rooted in an area around Valencia, Spain, paella is a classic one-pot dish: seafood, rice, and vegetables all cooked together. Though not a traditional Moroccan dish, it's a favorite of mine and I wanted to combine it with my favorite cooking method. So in this mash-up, the Spanish dish is slow-cooked in a Moroccan tagine with chermoula added to give the dish a burst of earthy, bright flavors. The choice of seafood is based on personal preference, which in my case is a combination of shrimp and white fish fillets, but you could also use clams or mussels.

1 pound large shrimp ($^{31}/_{35}$ count), peeled and deveined

10 ounces cod fillets, cut into 1½-inch pieces

3 tablespoons chermoula, homemade (page 175) or store-bought

2 cups jasmine or basmati rice, rinsed and soaked in water for 15 minutes and drained

3 tablespoons extra-virgin olive oil, divided, plus more for greasing the tagine

Kosher salt

Freshly ground black pepper

1 cup chopped bell pepper (any color)

½ cup chopped red onion

1 cup diced tomato, plus 5 tomato slices

2 limes, 1 cut into ⅓-inch-thick slices, 1 quartered

Boiling water

3 tablespoons salted butter, melted

1 lemon, cut into wedges

1. In a large bowl, combine the shrimp, cod, and 2 tablespoons of chermoula. Cover and marinate for 15 to 20 minutes.

2. In a large bowl, combine the rice, 2 tablespoons of olive oil, and remaining 1 tablespoon of chermoula. Season the rice with salt and pepper and set it aside.

3. Grease the inside of the tagine base with olive oil and place it on a diffuser over medium-low heat. Add the remaining 1 tablespoon of olive oil and sauté the bell pepper and onion for 7 minutes. Add the tomato and cook for 2 minutes. Spoon the mixture into the bowl with the rice, stirring to combine.

4. While the tagine is still on the heat, place the lime slices across the base, then add the rice mixture, gently leveling it. Put 4 cups of boiling water into the empty rice bowl, scraping the sides, and pour the water gently and evenly around the rice.

5. Cover the tagine and cook for 45 minutes, or until the rice is tender. Check the liquid level every 20 minutes and add boiling water by the tablespoon, as needed.

6. To the bowl with the marinated shrimp and cod, add the melted butter and squeeze in the juice from the lime wedges and mix well.

7. Uncover the tagine, arrange the shrimp and cod on the rice, and spread the rest of the marinade over the fish and rice. Cover and cook for about 20 minutes, or until the shrimp and fish are firm.

8. Set the tagine on a cooling rack to cool for 7 to 10 minutes. Serve with lemon wedges for squeezing.

COOKING TIP: Instead of cooking the marinated shrimp and fish in the tagine, sauté them in a little olive oil and butter for a bit of crispiness. Then add a squeeze of lemon, add it to the tagine, garnish, and serve.

Rolled Sole with Chermoula in Tomato Harissa Sauce

SERVES 4

PREP TIME:
30 minutes

COOK TIME:
45 minutes

Perfect for evenings when you want a quick family dinner, or when you need something special for lunch, this dish can come together in a snap—especially if the chermoula and tomato sauce have been made ahead. The sole can also be marinated overnight. Add roasted peppers or any other vegetables of choice to the tomato harissa sauce for extra flavor.

8 sole fillets (4 ounces each)

½ teaspoon kosher salt, divided

4 tablespoons chermoula, homemade (page 175) or store-bought, divided

1 large potato, grated, with the liquid squeezed out

1 cup whole pitted green olives, plus 3 tablespoons chopped

3 tablespoons extra-virgin olive oil

4 large tomatoes, chopped, or 2 (15-ounce) cans crushed tomatoes

1 tablespoon chopped fresh parsley, plus more for garnish

1 tablespoon chopped fresh cilantro

1 teaspoon harissa, homemade (page 174) or store-bought

Boiling water

1 lemon, cut into wedges

1. Place the sole fillets on a sheet pan, sprinkle them with ¼ teaspoon of salt, brush them all over with 2 tablespoons of chermoula, cover, and marinate for 10 minutes.

2. In a small bowl, combine the potato, 3 tablespoons of chopped olives, and 1 tablespoon of chermoula. Lay the sole on a clean cutting board and spread about 2 tablespoons of the potato mixture over each fillet, roll them up, and secure with toothpicks. Set them aside.

3. Place the tagine on a diffuser over medium-low heat. Grease the tagine with olive oil and heat for 2 minutes. Add the rolled fish to the tagine and cook for 2 to 3 minutes on each side, or until lightly browned, and transfer the fish to a clean plate.

4. Add the tomatoes, whole olives, remaining 1 tablespoon of chermoula, the parsley, cilantro, and harissa to the tagine, stirring to combine. Arrange the rolled sole on the tomato sauce, cover, and cook for 40 minutes, or until the fish is firm and the tomato sauce is slightly thick. Check the liquid level every 20 minutes and add boiling water by the tablespoon, as needed.

5. Set the tagine on a cooling rack to cool for 5 minutes. Garnish with parsley and serve with lemon wedges for squeezing.

COOKING TIP: This dish can also be cooked in the oven. Preheat the oven to 400°F, arrange everything in the tagine, drizzle the olive oil on the top of the rolled fish and tomato sauce, and cook it uncovered for 15 to 20 minutes.

CHAPTER 5

VEGETABLES

◄ **Chopped Kale with Roasted Garlic, Lemon, and Green Olives, 136**

Cauliflower, Onions, Garlic, Preserved Lemon, and Cilantro

PREP TIME:
15 minutes

COOK TIME:
40 minutes

The savory and intensely lemony addition of preserved lemon gives this vegan cauliflower tagine an incredible depth of flavor. Since this tagine dish is composed only of vegetables, it is best to go easy on the spices to avoid overwhelming the gentle flavor of the produce. It is a delicious main meal or a filling side dish for fish or barbecued meat.

¼ cup water

¼ cup chermoula, homemade (page 175) or store-bought

2 tablespoons extra-virgin olive oil, plus more for greasing the tagine

2 tablespoons chopped preserved lemon, homemade (page 172) or store-bought

2 garlic cloves, minced

½ teaspoon grated peeled fresh ginger

¼ teaspoon ground turmeric

1 large onion, cut into ¼-inch-thick slices

1 large tomato, finely chopped, or 1 cup canned diced tomatoes

1 head cauliflower, cut into medium florets

¼ teaspoon kosher salt

Boiling water

1 tablespoon chopped fresh cilantro, for garnish

1. In a small bowl, combine the water, chermoula, olive oil, preserved lemon, garlic, ginger, and turmeric to make a watery paste. Set the bowl aside.

2. Grease the inside of the tagine base with olive oil. Lay the onion slices across the base and top the onion with the tomato and cauliflower. Spread the spice mixture on the cauliflower and sprinkle with the salt.

3. Cover the tagine, place it on a diffuser over medium-low heat, and cook for 40 minutes, or until the cauliflower is tender-crisp and the sauce is creamy. Check the liquid level every 20 minutes and add boiling water by the tablespoon, as needed.

4. Set the tagine on a cooling rack to cool for 5 minutes. Serve garnished with cilantro.

SERVING TIP: As with all tagine cooking, taking the time to attractively arrange the vegetables creates a lovely presentation at the dinner table.

Green and Yellow Squash with Herbs

SERVES 4

PREP TIME:
15 minutes

COOK TIME:
40 minutes

Vegetarian tagines are popular in Morocco, and this is an extremely versatile example, with the combo of yellow and green squash making a lovely presentation. It's best to make this in the summer when squash have tender skin and flavorful flesh. Whenever possible, use in-season vegetables and fresh herbs.

¼ cup water

3 tablespoons chermoula, homemade (page 175) or store-bought

1 tablespoon extra-virgin olive oil

1 tablespoon Herb-Infused Oil (page 176), made with oregano (if unavailable, use extra-virgin olive oil)

½ teaspoon kosher salt

½ teaspoon dried oregano, divided

¼ teaspoon freshly ground black pepper

Olive oil for greasing the tagine

1 large onion, coarsely chopped

2 medium tomatoes, cut into ¼-inch-thick slices

2 green zucchini, cut on the diagonal into ⅓-inch-thick slices

2 yellow squash, cut on the diagonal into ⅓-inch-thick slices

Boiling water

½ cup chopped pitted Kalamata olives

1 tablespoon chopped fresh parsley, for garnish

1. In a small bowl, combine the water, chermoula, 1 tablespoon of olive oil, the herb-infused oil, salt, ¼ teaspoon of oregano, and the pepper to make a watery paste. Set the bowl aside.

2. Grease the inside of the tagine base with olive oil. Lay the onion across the base and top with half the tomato slices. Arrange half the zucchini and yellow squash slices over the tomatoes, then a final layer of tomato slices, and a final layer of zucchini and squash. Spread the spice mixture on the vegetables.

3. Cover the tagine, place it on a diffuser over medium-low heat, and cook for 25 minutes. Check the liquid level after 20 minutes and add boiling water by the tablespoon, as needed.

4. Uncover the tagine, distribute the olives over the vegetables, sprinkle with the remaining ¼ teaspoon of oregano, cover, and cook for 15 minutes longer, or until the squash and zucchini are tender-crisp and the sauce is creamy.

5. Set the tagine on a cooling rack to cool for 5 minutes. Serve garnished with parsley.

COOKING TIP: Squash, tomatoes, and onions usually release liquids while cooking, so be careful to not add too much water to this kind of tagine.

Chopped Kale with Roasted Garlic, Lemon, and Green Olives

SERVES 4

PREP TIME:
15 minutes

COOK TIME:
45 minutes

In Morocco, this dish is made with a leafy vegetable called *bakula* (mallow in English), which is a typical Moroccan salad green usually served as a side dish. Since this ingredient can be challenging to find outside North Africa, people often use spinach or kale instead. I like kale because its texture is like mallow and it is a wonderful superfood. This recipe is an excellent way to enjoy these healthy greens. Moroccan flavor is represented in every bite of these slow-cooked greens enhanced with chermoula, roasted garlic, olive oil, preserved lemon, and green olives.

¼ cup water

3 tablespoons chermoula, homemade (page 175) or store-bought

3 tablespoons extra-virgin olive oil, plus more for greasing the tagine

3 Roasted Garlic (page 173) cloves, minced

2 tablespoons tomato paste

1 tablespoon freshly squeezed lemon juice

1 tablespoon harissa, homemade (page 174) or store-bought

½ teaspoon kosher salt

1 large tomato, finely chopped, or 1 cup canned diced tomatoes

8 cups finely chopped kale leaves (stems and midribs removed)

Boiling water

1 cup pitted green olives, chopped, for garnish

¼ small preserved lemon, homemade (page 172) or store-bought, chopped, for garnish

1. In a small bowl, combine the water, chermoula, olive oil, roasted garlic, tomato paste, lemon juice, harissa, and salt to make a watery paste. Set the bowl aside.

2. Grease the inside of the tagine base with olive oil. Spread the tomato across the base and top with the kale. Pour the spice mixture over the vegetables and stir to combine.

3. Cover the tagine, place it on a diffuser over medium-low heat, and cook for 45 minutes, stirring halfway through, until the kale is very tender and the sauce is completely absorbed. Check the liquid level every 20 minutes and add boiling water by the tablespoon, as needed.

4. Set the tagine on a cooling rack to cool for 5 minutes. This dish is delicious served warm or cold. Serve garnished with olives and preserved lemon.

MAKE AHEAD: This dish can be made ahead and kept in an airtight container in the refrigerator for up for 5 days.

Artichoke Hearts and Green Peas with Garlic and Cilantro

SERVES 4

PREP TIME:
15 minutes

COOK TIME:
45 minutes

In Morocco, this artichoke and green pea tagine is traditionally cooked with meat. But you won't miss the meat because the earthy taste of artichoke goes so well with sweet green peas and preserved lemon; it is deliciously fragrant and very satisfying. You can add more vegetables to this dish, such as red potatoes, carrots, or green beans.

¼ cup water

3 tablespoons chopped fresh cilantro, divided

3 tablespoons chopped preserved lemon, homemade (page 172) or store-bought

2 tablespoons extra-virgin olive oil, plus more for greasing the tagine

4 garlic cloves, minced

¾ teaspoon kosher salt

½ teaspoon grated peeled fresh ginger

½ teaspoon ground turmeric

¼ teaspoon freshly ground black pepper

2 medium onions, cut into ¼-inch-thick slices

1 medium tomato, finely chopped, or ½ cup canned diced tomatoes

8 medium artichoke hearts, fresh, frozen, or canned

2 cups green peas, fresh or frozen

Boiling water

1. In a small bowl, combine the water, 2 tablespoons of cilantro, the preserved lemon, olive oil, garlic, salt, ginger, turmeric, and pepper to make a watery paste. Set the bowl aside.

2. Grease the inside of the tagine base with olive oil. Lay the onion slices across the base, top with tomato, arrange the artichoke hearts on the tomatoes, and fill in the spaces with the peas. Spread the spice mixture on the vegetables.

3. Cover the tagine, place it on a diffuser over medium-low heat, and cook for 45 minutes, or until the artichoke hearts are tender and the sauce is creamy. Check the liquid level every 20 minutes and add boiling water by the tablespoon, as needed.

4. Set the tagine on a cooling rack to cool for 5 minutes. Serve garnished with the remaining 1 tablespoon of cilantro.

COOKING TIP: If you want to adjust the seasoning levels of a dish, don't do it until the last 15 minutes of cooking. If you do it too early, when the dish's flavors have yet to concentrate, you risk overseasoning the food.

White Beans, Tomatoes, Herbs, and Harissa

SERVES 4

PREP TIME:
15 minutes

COOK TIME:
45 minutes

Creamy, savory, and satisfying, this vegan stew—which features slow-cooked white beans in olive oil, herbs, and harissa—is a very popular dish in Morocco. It can also be cooked with meat, sausage, or bone marrow, and all kinds of greens, such as spinach, mustard greens, baby kale, or collard greens. It is perfect for cold wintery evenings.

4 tablespoons extra-virgin olive oil, divided

1 large onion, finely chopped

½ cup thinly sliced leeks

4 garlic cloves, minced

2 large tomatoes, finely chopped, or 2 cups canned diced tomatoes

3 cups cooked white beans (see Tip), such as cannellini, or 2 (15-ounce) cans white beans, drained and rinsed

3 tablespoons chopped fresh cilantro, divided

2 tablespoons harissa, homemade (page 174) or store-bought

2 sprigs fresh or dried thyme, or 1 teaspoon dried thyme

¾ teaspoon kosher salt

½ teaspoon grated peeled fresh ginger

½ teaspoon ground turmeric

¼ teaspoon freshly ground black pepper

½ cup water

Boiling water

1. Place 2 tablespoons of olive oil in the tagine base and set on a diffuser over medium-low heat. Heat the olive oil for 2 minutes, then add the onion and leeks and sauté for about 5 minutes, until lightly caramelized. Add the garlic and sauté for 2 minutes, or until fragrant. Add the tomatoes and sauté for 30 seconds.

2. Add the beans, 2 tablespoons of cilantro, remaining 2 tablespoons of olive oil, the harissa, thyme, salt, ginger, turmeric, and pepper and stir to combine. Stir in the water.

3. Cover the tagine and cook for 40 minutes, or until the beans are tender and the sauce is creamy. Check the liquid level every 20 minutes and add boiling water by the table-spoon, as needed.

4. Set the tagine on a cooling rack to cool for 5 minutes. Serve garnished with the remaining 1 tablespoon of cilantro.

MAKE AHEAD: If you want to start from dried beans instead of using canned, cook them up to several days ahead. First, soak the dried beans overnight, then drain, rinse, and slow-cook in lots of salted water until tender.

STORAGE TIP: This tagine freezes well, so you can always have a prepared meal handy to reheat. Cook the tagine, let it cool, then transfer to a zip-top bag or freezer-safe glass container and freeze for up to 1 month.

Lentil, Garlic, Celery, Kale, and Butternut Squash

SERVES 4

PREP TIME:
15 minutes,
plus 1 hour
to soak
the lentils

COOK TIME:
50 minutes

Lentil stew does not take much time to cook, but it does require a bit of supervision to get the ideal legume texture. You need to add enough liquid so the lentils are not hard, but not too much or cook them too long or they will be mushy. Butternut squash adds a wonderful sweetness to this dish, and the celery and kale provide a satisfying salty and savory flavor—perfectly balanced!

3 tablespoons extra-virgin olive oil, divided

1 large onion, finely chopped

½ cup finely chopped celery

4 garlic cloves, minced

1 large tomato, finely diced, or 1 cup canned diced tomatoes

3 cups dried lentils (brown or green), soaked in water for 1 hour, drained, and rinsed

1 cup chopped baby kale leaves

1 cup diced butternut squash

2 tablespoons chopped fresh cilantro, divided

¾ teaspoon kosher salt, plus more as desired

½ teaspoon grated peeled fresh ginger

½ teaspoon ground turmeric

¼ teaspoon freshly ground black pepper

2 cups water

Boiling water

1. Place 2 tablespoons of olive oil in the tagine base and set on a diffuser over medium-low heat. Heat the oil for 2 minutes, then add the onion and sauté for about 5 minutes, or until lightly caramelized. Add the celery and garlic and sauté for 2 minutes, or until fragrant. Add the tomatoes and sauté for 30 seconds.

2. Add the lentils, kale, butternut squash, 1 tablespoon of cilantro, remaining 1 tablespoon of olive oil, the salt, ginger, turmeric, and pepper and stir to combine. Stir in the water.

3. Cover the tagine and cook for about 45 minutes, or until the lentils are tender and the sauce is creamy. Check the liquid level every 20 minutes and add boiling water by the tablespoon, as needed.

4. Set the tagine on a cooling rack to cool for 5 minutes. Serve garnished with the remaining 1 tablespoon of cilantro.

MAKE AHEAD: The lentils can be cooked ahead in salted water after they are soaked and kept in the refrigerator in an airtight container for up to 4 days.

Eggplant and Tomatoes with Roasted Garlic, Lemon, and Cilantro

Warm, hearty, and vegan, this is a simple, flavorful Moroccan stew of caramelized eggplant and onions in a lemony roasted garlic tomato sauce. It can be made ahead and enjoyed as leftovers because it gets even more delicious as the flavors have time to meld. This eggplant marmalade is also ideal for adding to sandwiches.

3 tablespoons extra-virgin olive oil, divided, plus more for drizzling

2 large eggplant, peeled and cut into 1-inch cubes

½ teaspoon kosher salt, divided

½ medium onion, finely chopped

4 Roasted Garlic (page 173) cloves, minced

2 large tomatoes, finely diced, or 2 cups canned diced tomatoes

¼ small preserved lemon, homemade (page 172) or store-bought, chopped, plus more for garnish

2 tablespoons freshly squeezed lemon juice

2 tablespoons chopped fresh cilantro, divided

½ teaspoon ground cumin

½ teaspoon sweet paprika

Boiling water

1. Place 2 tablespoons of olive oil in the tagine base and set on a diffuser over medium-low heat. Heat the oil for 2 minutes, then add the eggplant and ¼ teaspoon of salt and sauté for about 5 minutes, until lightly caramelized. Add the onion and roasted garlic and sauté for 2 minutes, or until fragrant.

2. Add the tomatoes, preserved lemon, lemon juice, 1 tablespoon of cilantro, remaining 1 tablespoon of olive oil, the cumin, paprika, and remaining ¼ teaspoon of salt and stir to combine.

3. Cover the tagine and cook for 40 minutes, or until all the ingredients are well combined and thick. Check the liquid level every 20 minutes and add boiling water by the tablespoon, as needed.

4. Set the tagine on a cooling rack to cool for 5 minutes. Serve with a drizzle of olive oil and garnished with preserved lemon and the remaining 1 tablespoon of cilantro.

SERVING TIP: Serve this as an appetizer with slices of cheese on crackers or a slice of crusty baguette, or as a side dish next to grilled meat, chicken, or fish.

Chickpeas, Roasted Garlic, and Cilantro

SERVES 4

PREP TIME:
15 minutes

COOK TIME:
45 minutes

Serve this as a side dish, or elevate it to a vegan main dish by adding vegetables, such as carrots and butternut squash, and serving it over Fluffy Couscous (page 170) or rice. In Morocco, this chickpea tagine is actually often cooked with meat to make it a main dish. Raisins or any dried fruit add complementary sweetness to this dish, or you can take in a spicy direction by throwing in chiles or harissa.

3 tablespoons extra-virgin olive oil, divided

1 large onion, finely chopped

4 Roasted Garlic (page 173) cloves, minced

1 medium tomato, finely chopped, or ½ cup canned diced tomatoes

3 cups cooked chickpeas (see Tip) or 2 (15-ounce) cans chickpeas, drained and rinsed

1 cinnamon stick

1 teaspoon ras el hanout, homemade (page 15) or store-bought

¾ teaspoon kosher salt

½ teaspoon ground cumin

Pinch saffron threads

Boiling water

2 tablespoons chopped fresh cilantro

1. Place 2 tablespoons of olive oil in the tagine base and set on a diffuser over medium-low heat. Heat the oil for 2 minutes, then add the onion and sauté for about 5 minutes, or until lightly caramelized. Add the roasted garlic and sauté for 2 minutes, or until fragrant. Add the tomato and sauté for 30 seconds.

2. Add the chickpeas, remaining 1 tablespoon of olive oil, the cinnamon stick, ras el hanout, salt, cumin, and saffron and stir to combine.

3. Cover the tagine and cook for 40 minutes, or until the chickpeas are tender and the sauce is creamy. Check the liquid level every 20 minutes and add boiling water by the tablespoon, as needed.

4. Set the tagine on a cooling rack to cool for 5 minutes. Discard the cinnamon stick, stir in the cilantro, and serve.

MAKE AHEAD: Smaller dried chickpeas taste better than the big ones, even canned, so always choose the small ones, if possible. Soak the beans overnight, then drain, rinse, and cook them in salted water over medium-low heat. Cool the chickpeas and freeze them in an airtight container for up to 1 month.

Mixed Veggies with Preserved Lemon

SERVES 4

PREP TIME:
15 minutes

COOK TIME:
40 minutes

Use any seasonal vegetables you may have on hand for this amazing vegetarian family favorite. What makes these humble ingredients stand out is simmering them in a tagine with fragrant spices and preserved lemon. The complex flavors of this dish come from layering the ingredients in the tagine, then gently slow-cooking them to perfection. For a hearty meal, serve this dish with crunchy bread, spicy olives, and fresh green salad.

½ cup water, divided

¼ small preserved lemon, homemade (page 172) or store-bought, finely chopped, plus more for garnish

4 garlic cloves, minced

2 tablespoons extra-virgin olive oil, plus more for greasing the tagine

2 tablespoons chopped fresh cilantro, divided

½ teaspoon kosher salt

1 teaspoon Karima's Beef Spice Mix (page 177)

1 large onion, diced

1 large tomato, diced, or 1 cup canned diced tomatoes

2 large potatoes, peeled and cut into 4 lengthwise pieces, or 4 medium red potatoes, halved

4 medium carrots, quartered lengthwise

2 cups green peas, fresh or frozen

2 cups green beans

Boiling water

1. In a small bowl, combine ¼ cup of water, the preserved lemon, garlic, olive oil, 1 tablespoon of cilantro, the salt, and spice mix to make a watery paste. Set the bowl aside.

2. Grease the inside of the tagine base with olive oil, spread the onion across the base, and top with the tomato. Arrange the potatoes and carrots in a conical shape in the

center and add the peas and green beans. Spread the spice mixture over the vegetables. Add the remaining ¼ cup of water to the bowl, swirl, and pour it around the edges of the base.

3. Cover the tagine, place it on a diffuser over medium-low heat, and cook for 40 minutes, or until the vegetables are very tender and the sauce is creamy. Check the liquid level every 20 minutes and add boiling water by the tablespoon, as needed.

4. Set the tagine on a cooling rack to cool for 5 minutes. Serve garnished with the remaining 1 tablespoon of cilantro.

VARIATION: If you want to boost the flavor and heat of this dish, add some harissa and olives.

MAKE AHEAD: This dish will taste even better the next day, so either make it a day ahead, or make sure you save some leftovers!

Stuffed Zucchini in Spicy Herb Tomato Sauce

SERVES 4

PREP TIME:
25 minutes

COOK TIME:
1 hour

Zucchini is the classic choice for stuffing, but this vegetable side dish (or appetizer) could also be made with eggplant, bell peppers, tomatoes, or potatoes. This wonderful dish also makes great leftovers, because the longer it sits (up to 4 days in the refrigerator), the more flavors it absorbs.

2 large potatoes, grated, rinsed, and liquid squeezed out

½ cup finely chopped celery

1 large egg, beaten

3 tablespoons chermoula, homemade (page 175) or store-bought, divided

3 tablespoons extra-virgin olive oil, divided, plus more for greasing the tagine

½ teaspoon kosher salt, divided

4 large zucchini

3 large tomatoes, finely diced, or 3 cups canned diced tomatoes

1 teaspoon chopped fresh oregano

1 medium onion, finely diced

Boiling water

1 tablespoon chopped fresh cilantro, for garnish

1. In a large bowl, combine the potatoes, celery, egg, 2 tablespoons of chermoula, 1 tablespoon of olive oil, and ¼ teaspoon of salt. Set the bowl aside.

2. Halve the zucchini lengthwise and use a spoon to scoop out the flesh, leaving a ¼-inch-thick wall all around.

3. Evenly divide the potato mixture among the zucchini halves.

4. In a medium bowl, combine the tomatoes, oregano, 1 tablespoon of olive oil, remaining 1 tablespoon of chermoula, and remaining ¼ teaspoon of salt.

5. Grease the inside of the tagine base with olive oil. Spread the onion across the base and top with the diced tomatoes. Arrange the zucchini halves in the tomato sauce and drizzle with the remaining 1 tablespoon of olive oil.

6. Cover the tagine, place it on a diffuser over medium-low heat, and cook for 1 hour, or until the zucchini is tender and the sauce is thick. Check the liquid level every 20 minutes and add boiling water by the tablespoon, as needed.

7. Set the tagine on a cooling rack to cool for 5 minutes. Serve garnished with cilantro.

VARIATION: To turn this appetizer into a main course, add any protein to the filling mixture or some shredded cheese as a tasty topping.

Roasted Bell Pepper, Tomato, and Roasted Garlic Shakshuka

SERVES 4

PREP TIME:
15 minutes

COOK TIME:
35 minutes

With a unique smokiness from ground cumin, this roasted red pepper, tomato, and egg dish is easy to make. Serve it for any meal during the day—breakfast, lunch, or dinner. It is wonderful with oil-cured black olives, fresh mozzarella or goat cheese, and crusty fresh bread. In Morocco, we call this dish *taktouka*.

2 tablespoons extra-virgin olive oil, plus more for drizzling

1 medium onion, finely chopped

4 Roasted Garlic (page 173) cloves, or fresh, minced

3 large tomatoes, finely diced, or 3 cups canned diced tomatoes

3 roasted red peppers, chopped

2 tablespoons chopped fresh parsley, divided

1 tablespoon chopped fresh cilantro

¾ teaspoon ground cumin, divided

½ teaspoon sweet paprika

½ teaspoon kosher salt

8 large eggs

1. Place the olive in the tagine base and set on a diffuser over medium-low heat. Heat the olive oil for 2 minutes, then add the onion and sauté for about 5 minutes or until lightly browned. Add the roasted garlic and sauté for 2 minutes, or until fragrant.

2. Add the tomatoes, roasted peppers, 1 tablespoon of parsley, the cilantro, ½ teaspoon of cumin, the paprika, and salt and stir to combine.

3. Cover the tagine and cook for 20 minutes, or until the sauce is thick.

4. Uncover the tagine and crack the eggs into the sauce, leaving some space between them, cover, and cook for 6 to 8 minutes, until the whites are set.

5. Set the tagine on a cooling rack to cool for 5 minutes. Serve with a drizzle of oil and sprinkled with the remaining ¼ teaspoon cumin and 1 tablespoon of parsley.

MAKE AHEAD: You can make the sauce for this dish and after it cools, store it covered in the refrigerator. When ready to eat, let the tagine come to room temperature, warm the dish in the tagine, then crack in the eggs.

VARIATION: Try this dish with a sausage side or sprinkled with shredded cheese.

Caramelized Tomato, Honey, and Sesame Seeds

SERVES 4

PREP TIME:
10 minutes

COOK TIME:
1 hour
10 minutes

Roasting tomatoes in the tagine concentrates the flavors intensely and creates firmly textured, juicy caramelized tomatoes. These caramelized tomatoes are delicious by themselves but can also enhance other recipes, such as soups, appetizers, or as a garnish. They work incredibly well with lamb, beef, or chicken tagine, saffron basmati rice, Fluffy Couscous (page 170), salads, and cheesy scrambled eggs.

3 tablespoons extra-virgin olive oil, divided, plus more for greasing the tagine

1 medium onion, finely chopped

6 Roasted Garlic cloves (page 173), or fresh

4 large tomatoes, cut into 1-inch-thick slices

½ teaspoon kosher salt

2 teaspoons chopped fresh thyme

1 teaspoon ras el hanout, homemade (page 15) or store-bought

Pinch ground nutmeg

2 teaspoons honey

Boiling water

1 tablespoon toasted sesame seeds, for garnish

1. Preheat the oven to 375°F.

2. Place 2 tablespoons of olive oil in the tagine base and set on a diffuser over medium-low heat. Heat the olive oil for 2 minutes, then add the onion and sauté for about 5 minutes, or until lightly browned.

3. Remove the tagine from the heat, add the roasted garlic, and arrange the tomato slices, working from the center out in an attractive presentation. Sprinkle with the salt, thyme, ras el hanout, and nutmeg. Drizzle with the remaining 1 tablespoon of olive oil and the honey.

4. Transfer the uncovered tagine to the oven and bake for 1 hour, or until the tomatoes caramelize. Check the liquid level every 20 minutes and add boiling water by the tablespoon, as needed.

5. Set the tagine on a cooling rack to cool for 5 minutes. Serve garnished with sesame seeds.

STORAGE TIP: Leftover tomatoes stay fresh in an airtight container in the refrigerator for up to 4 days.

Spicy Cabbage-Stuffed Potatoes in Tomato Sauce

SERVES 4

PREP TIME:
25 minutes

COOK TIME:
1 hour

Unlike other "loaded potato" recipes, this version stuffs filling into an *unbaked* potato. These potatoes are a wonderful side dish with everything from roast chicken to meat kebabs or fish. They're also a hearty appetizer.

3 large potatoes

3 cups finely chopped green cabbage

2 cups shredded carrots

1 cup chopped pitted black olives

3 tablespoons chermoula, homemade (page 175) or store-bought, divided

3 tablespoons extra-virgin olive oil, divided, plus more for brushing

1 teaspoon kosher salt, divided

½ teaspoon freshly ground black pepper, divided

3 cups finely chopped tomatoes, or 3 cups canned diced tomatoes

1 large onion, diced

Boiling water

2 tablespoons chopped scallions, white and green parts, for garnish

1. Peel the potatoes, halve them lengthwise, and scoop out the flesh with a melon baller, leaving a ¼-inch wall all around. Chop the scooped-out flesh and place in a large bowl.

2. To the large bowl with the potato flesh, add the cabbage, carrots, olives, 2 tablespoons of chermoula, 1 tablespoon of olive oil, ½ teaspoon of salt, and ¼ teaspoon of pepper. Set the bowl aside.

3. In a medium bowl, combine the tomatoes, 1 tablespoon of olive oil, ¼ teaspoon of salt, and remaining 1 tablespoon of chermoula. Set the bowl aside.

4. Brush the potato halves all over with olive oil and season with the remaining ½ teaspoon of salt and ¼ teaspoon of pepper. Evenly divide the cabbage mixture among the potato halves.

5. Brush the inside of the tagine base with olive oil. Spread the onion across the base and top with the tomato mixture. Arrange the potatoes on the tomatoes and drizzle with the remaining 1 tablespoon of olive oil.

6. Cover the tagine, place it on a diffuser over medium-low heat, and cook for 1 hour, or until the potato halves are tender and the sauce is thick. Check the liquid level every 20 minutes and add boiling water by the tablespoon, as needed.

7. Set the tagine on a cooling rack to cool for 5 minutes. Serve garnished with scallions.

COOKING TIP: This dish can also be baked in a preheated oven at 350°F if you want a crispier potato.

MAKE AHEAD: This might look like a complicated dish, but it isn't if you do a little advance prep. To make it easier, make the filling and tomato sauce ahead.

Bulgur, Carrot, and Herb Stuffed Bell Peppers

SERVES 4

PREP TIME:
25 minutes,
plus
20 minutes
to soak
the bulgur

COOK TIME:
1 hour

This stuffed pepper tagine is worth the preparation time. It can be made ahead and refrigerated in an airtight container for up to 4 days to accommodate last-minute dinner decisions. You can also set it up in the tagine, cover it, and refrigerate it to cook the next day. Remember to bring the tagine to room temperature before cooking to avoid cracking it! This tagine is a wonderful side dish or appetizer, but you can add ground meat or chicken to make it a dinner entrée. Leftover cooked quinoa or rice work well instead of bulgur.

2 cups bulgur, soaked for 20 minutes in cold water, and drained

2 cups shredded carrots

2 cups chopped roasted red peppers

3 tablespoons extra-virgin olive oil, plus more for brushing the green peppers and greasing the tagine

3 tablespoons chermoula, homemade (page 175) or store-bought, divided

1 teaspoon kosher salt, divided

3 cups finely chopped tomatoes or 3 cups canned diced tomatoes

½ teaspoon ground cumin, divided

3 large bell peppers (any color), halved lengthwise and seeded

1 large onion, diced

Boiling water

2 tablespoons chopped pitted green olives, for garnish

1. Preheat the oven to 350°F.

2. In a large bowl, combine the bulgur, carrots, roasted peppers, 1 tablespoon of olive oil, 2 tablespoons of chermoula, and ½ teaspoon of salt. Set the bowl aside.

3. In a medium bowl, combine the tomatoes, 1 tablespoon of olive oil, ¼ teaspoon of salt, and remaining 1 tablespoon of chermoula. Set the bowl aside.

4. Cut the bell peppers lengthwise (through the stem; see Tip) and pull out the ribs and seeds. Brush the bell peppers all over with olive oil and season them with ¼ teaspoon of cumin and the remaining ¼ teaspoon of salt. Evenly divide the bulgur mixture among the pepper halves.

5. Grease the inside of the tagine base with olive oil. Spread the onion across the base and top with the tomato mixture. Arrange the stuffed peppers on the tomatoes, drizzle with the remaining 1 tablespoon of olive oil, and sprinkle with the remaining ¼ teaspoon of cumin.

6. Transfer the uncovered tagine to the oven and cook for 1 hour, or until the peppers are tender and the sauce is creamy. Check the liquid level every 20 minutes and add boiling water by the tablespoon, as needed.

7. Set the tagine on a cooling rack to cool for 10 minutes. Serve garnished with chopped olives.

SERVING TIP: You have two presentation choices for the peppers. Cut them lengthwise through the stem when you are also serving other stuffed vegetables like zucchini or eggplant, so they look alike. Or just cut the tops off and cook them upright when you are serving them with stuffed potatoes and tomatoes for an elegant presentation. Both look amazing and will hold the filling equally well.

Seven-Vegetable Tagine

SERVES 4

PREP TIME:
15 minutes

COOK TIME:
1 hour

Packed with warm Moroccan spices and heaps of flavorful vegetables, this vibrant and colorful dish is fit for special company. Based on a popular Moroccan couscous dish—which has, you guessed it, seven vegetables—the trick is to arrange the vegetables in a conical shape so the juice from each drips over the others. However, the dish requires a deep tagine to hold enough liquid to cook the vegetables. If you have a shallower vessel, reduce the quantity of each vegetable so you benefit from the tastes and flavors of all seven without overflowing the tagine.

½ cup water, divided

3 tablespoons extra-virgin olive oil, plus more for greasing the tagine

2 tablespoons chopped fresh cilantro, divided

1½ teaspoons Karima's Beef Spice Mix (page 177)

½ teaspoon kosher salt

1 large onion, diced

1 large tomato, diced, or 1 cup canned diced tomatoes

2 cups thick-sliced green cabbage

2 medium carrots, quartered lengthwise

2 medium zucchini, halved lengthwise

1 medium turnip, peeled and cut into 8 wedges

6 half-moon slices (¼ inch thick) peeled butternut squash

Boiling water

1. In a small bowl, combine ¼ cup of water, the olive oil, 1 tablespoon of cilantro, the spice mix, and salt to make a watery paste. Set the bowl aside.

2. Grease the inside of the tagine base with olive oil. Spread the onion across the base and top with the tomato. Arrange the vegetables in a conical shape in the center in the following order: cabbage, carrots, zucchini, turnip, and

butternut squash. Spread the spice mixture on the vegetables. Put the remaining ¼ cup of water into the empty spice paste bowl, swirl, and pour it around the edges of the tagine.

3. Cover the tagine, place it on a diffuser over medium-low heat, and cook for 1 hour, or until the vegetables are tender and the sauce is thick. Check the liquid level every 20 minutes and add boiling water by the tablespoon, as needed.

4. Set the tagine on a cooling rack to cool for 5 minutes. Serve garnished with the remaining 1 tablespoon of cilantro.

Quince, Caramelized Onion, and Raisins

SERVES 4

PREP TIME:
15 minutes

COOK TIME:
1 hour

Naturally sweet from slow-cooked caramelized onions and golden raisins and tart from the quince, this flavor combination is what makes Moroccan cuisine famous. Try this vegan dish served over quinoa, basmati saffron rice, or Fluffy Couscous (page 170). Or arrange your dinner table with traditional accompaniments of spicy olives, roasted pepper Moroccan salad, and crusty bread.

¼ cup water

3 tablespoons extra-virgin olive oil, divided

4 garlic cloves, minced

1 tablespoon chopped fresh cilantro

1 teaspoon ras el hanout, homemade (page 15) or store-bought, or Karima's Lamb Spice Mix (page 178)

½ teaspoon kosher salt

¼ teaspoon ground cinnamon

Pinch saffron threads

2 medium onions, cut into ¼-inch-thick slices

Boiling water

3 medium quince, quartered lengthwise

½ cup golden raisins

½ cup toasted chopped almonds, for garnish

1. In a small bowl, combine the water, 2 tablespoons of olive oil, the garlic, cilantro, ras el hanout, salt, cinnamon, and saffron to make a watery paste. Set the bowl aside.

2. Place the remaining 1 tablespoon of olive oil in the tagine base and set on a diffuser over medium-low heat. Heat the oil for 2 minutes, then arrange the onion slices in an even layer in the base. Spread half the spice mixture on the onions.

3. Cover the tagine and cook for 30 minutes, or until the onions start caramelizing. Check the liquid level every 15 minutes and add boiling water by the tablespoon, as needed.

4. Uncover the tagine, arrange the quince wedges on the onions, sprinkle on the raisins, and spoon the remaining spice mixture over everything. Cover and cook for about 30 minutes longer, or until the quinces are tender and the sauce creamy.

5. Set the tagine on a cooling rack to cool for 5 minutes. Serve garnished with almonds.

COOKING TIP: The spice mixture is supposed to be somewhat watery, so it sticks to the vegetables but also trickles between them through the layers.

Tagine Omelet

SERVES 4

PREP TIME:
10 minutes

COOK TIME:
20 minutes

In this recipe, the base of a tagine is used much like a skillet to sauté eggs and vegetables into a soft, open-faced omelet. You can make this egg tagine with various vegetables, such as bell peppers, onions, mushrooms, spinach, scallions, potatoes, zucchini, or chopped tomatoes. Other possible toppings for this dish include chives or mozzarella cheese.

2 tablespoons extra-virgin olive oil, divided

1 cup finely chopped onions

1 cup chopped bell peppers (any color)

6 large eggs, beaten

2 tablespoons finely chopped fresh parsley (optional)

½ teaspoon kosher salt

¼ teaspoon freshly ground black pepper

¼ teaspoon ground cumin

½ cup crumbled goat or feta cheese

1. Place 1 tablespoon of olive oil in the tagine base and set it on a diffuser over medium-low heat. Heat the olive oil for 2 minutes, then add the onions and bell peppers and sauté for 5 to 7 minutes, until lightly browned.

2. In a medium bowl, whisk together the eggs, parsley (if using), salt, and black pepper until fluffy. Pour the eggs evenly over the vegetables and drizzle with the remaining 1 tablespoon of olive oil. Cook for 8 to 10 minutes, using a wooden spatula to gently lift the edges to let the uncooked egg flow underneath, until the eggs are cooked yet moist.

3. Take the tagine off the heat. Transfer the omelet to a serving dish, sprinkle with cumin, and top with feta.

COOKING TIP: Remove the omelet from the tagine immediately after it is done because the heat from the tagine base will keep cooking the eggs. If you want to serve in the tagine, place the tagine (omelet still in it) on a folded towel to cool it down quickly.

Fava Beans with Eggs

PREP TIME:
15 minutes

COOK TIME:
25 minutes

Cracking the eggs directly into a delicious jalapeño-enhanced sauce creates a beautiful presentation, perfect for a special family breakfast or lunch served with fresh bread or pita.

2 tablespoons extra-virgin olive oil, divided

1 cup finely chopped onions

2 teaspoons chopped seeded jalapeño pepper

1 (15-ounce) can fava beans, drained and rinsed

1 cup finely chopped tomatoes

3 tablespoons chopped fresh cilantro, divided

½ teaspoon garlic powder

½ teaspoon kosher salt, divided

½ teaspoon ground cumin, divided

¼ teaspoon sweet paprika

6 large eggs, beaten

1. Place 1 tablespoon of oil in the tagine base and set on a diffuser over medium-low heat for 2 minutes. Then add the onions and jalapeño and sauté for 5 to 7 minutes, until lightly browned.

2. Add the beans, tomatoes, 2 tablespoons of cilantro, garlic powder, ¼ teaspoon of salt, ¼ teaspoon of cumin, and the paprika. Stir and let it cook for 15 minutes, or until the tomatoes are soft and the sauce is thick.

3. In a medium bowl, whisk the eggs with the remaining ¼ teaspoon of salt and pour it evenly over the fava bean mixture. Use a wooden spatula to gently move the eggs around and cook until the eggs are cooked yet moist.

4. Remove the tagine immediately from the heat and place it on a folded kitchen towel to cool it off and stop cooking. Serve sprinkled with the remaining ¼ teaspoon of cumin and 1 tablespoon of cilantro.

INGREDIENT TIP: Look for fava beans without added spices.

CHAPTER 6

STAPLES

◄ Tagine Baked Bread, 168

Tagine Baked Bread

SERVES 2

PREP TIME:
15 minutes,
plus 1 hour
40 minutes
to rise

COOK TIME:
20 minutes

Bread is a staple addition for tagine meals to ensure you can scoop up every drop of the delectable sauces. This easy recipe has only six ingredients and produces a fresh, warm, aromatic bread for breakfast or any meal. This bread has a crunchy crust and moist center, no preservatives, and a great taste.

1¼ cups warm water, divided

1 teaspoon active dry yeast

2 cups sifted unbleached all-purpose flour, whole-wheat flour, or barley flour, plus more for sprinkling

¾ teaspoon kosher salt

½ teaspoon fennel seeds or anise seeds, plus more (optional) for sprinkling

1 teaspoon honey (optional)

Olive oil, for rubbing the dough and greasing the tagine

1. In a small bowl, mix ¼ cup of warm water and the yeast and set aside for 10 minutes.

2. In a large bowl, mix the flour, salt, and seeds. Add the yeast mixture and honey (if using). Add some of the remaining 1 cup of warm water a little at the time, while mixing with a wooden spoon, to get a soft dough.

3. Knead the dough for 1 minute with your hands, form it into a ball, and rub it with some olive oil. Set the dough in the bowl, cover with a kitchen towel, and set it aside in a warm area to rise for about 1 hour, or until doubled.

4. Grease the inside of the tagine base with olive oil. Line with parchment paper and generously sprinkle flour all over the paper.

5. Lightly flour a work surface and turn the dough out. Shape it into a flattened ball and fold the dough into the center from all four sides, pressing each fold. Then shape it back into a ball and flatten it into a 1-inch-thick disc that will fit in the tagine base, transfer it to the tagine, sprinkle with seeds (if using), then press with your hands to flatten it. Cover the tagine with a cloth and leave the dough to rise for 40 minutes, or until it increases in volume by half.

6. Position a rack in the upper third of the oven and preheat the oven to 400°F.

7. Transfer the uncovered tagine to the oven and bake for 15 to 20 minutes, until the crust of the bread is hard and lightly browned. Transfer the bread to a kitchen towel to cool off completely before cutting it.

COOKING TIP: If your bread doesn't seem to be rising quickly enough, move it to a warmer space. I like a spot near the stove, or when the weather is cold, I place the tagine in the oven with just the light on. This is just warm enough to create a perfect proofing area.

Fluffy Couscous

SERVES 2

PREP TIME:
15 minutes

COOK TIME:
30 minutes

I was never satisfied with the results when following the box instructions of instant couscous, so I developed this tagine method, which produces fluffy, light couscous every time. When I was growing up, couscous was steamed three times in a pot called a couscoussier: a two-part vessel with a special perforated steamer insert that sits over a larger pot of cooking meat or vegetables (or just boiling water). Using a tagine as a tool to slow-steam couscous years later, I got a lovely result, closer to using that traditional steamer. Although couscous is not usually served with tagines, it is a great accompaniment for certain recipes like the Seven-Vegetable Tagine (page 160), which is especially saucy.

1 cup couscous (not instant)

1 tablespoon extra-virgin olive oil, plus more for greasing the tagine and for drizzling

1½ cups water, plus 2 tablespoons, divided

¼ teaspoon kosher salt

1 tablespoon unsalted butter, cut into small cubes

1. Place the couscous in a medium bowl, drizzle it with the olive oil, and use your hands to mix it so every grain of couscous is coated with oil.

2. Add 1 cup of water and the salt and mix gently. Set the couscous aside for 2 to 3 minutes to absorb the water. Mix with a fork, add another ½ cup of water, and set it aside for 3 minutes.

3. Preheat the oven to 350°F. Grease the inside of the tagine base with olive oil.

4. Fluff up the couscous with a fork to break up all the clumps, then transfer the couscous to the tagine base, spreading it out evenly. Cover the couscous tightly with parchment paper and then aluminum foil, crimping the foil around the edges.

5. Transfer the tagine to the oven and bake the couscous for 30 minutes, or until it is fluffy and the grains double in volume. If the grains are not tender, mix in a final 2 tablespoons of water and return to the oven to finish steaming.

6. Transfer the couscous to a serving bowl, adjust the salt, and add the butter. If desired, drizzle with a bit of olive oil. Gently fluff the couscous with a fork and serve.

COOKING TIP: Make sure the parchment paper (or foil) is secured well or the steam will escape and the couscous will be dry and slightly crunchy on top.

Preserved Lemon

MAKES
6 LEMONS

PREP TIME:
15 minutes,
plus 5 to
6 weeks to
preserve

Preserved lemons are essential to Moroccan cuisine. They are used to add salt and depth to tagines, stews, dressings, sauces, dips, baking, and endless savory dishes. Preserved lemons are salted and packed into a jar where they ferment for several weeks to several months. These tasty, pickled lemons add flavor and acidity to slow-cooked tagine dishes. When pureed into a paste, they are a delicious addition to cake batter, cookie dough, custard, and ice cream.

6 lemons

½ cup kosher salt, plus more
  as needed

Water

1. Quarter each lemon by cutting lengthwise toward the stem end, but not cutting all the way through so the lemon is still attached at the bottom. Pull the quarters open like the petals of a flower. Press the salt on all the cut edges, then hold the lemon cupped in your hand, with the open part facing up, and fill the crevices with salt. Press the lemon quarters together and place it in a large canning jar.

2. Repeat until all the lemons are salted and squeezed into the jar. Pour in enough water to cover them, add 1 tablespoon of salt, seal the jar tightly, and store in a cool area for 5 to 6 weeks.

COOKING TIP: Check the preserved lemons once a week, flipping the jar a few times so the liquid reaches all of them.

Roasted Garlic

PREP TIME:
5 minutes

COOK TIME:
20 minutes

Roasting garlic in the oven brings out its unique flavor and creamy texture, perfect for adding heaps of flavor to meals. These sweet, buttery, caramelized garlic cloves can be added to any dish and are an essential staple to keep on hand. Try these mellow cloves with roasted, steamed, or sautéed vegetables; on baked potatoes; spreads for bread; on pasta; and in dips or vinaigrettes.

1 tablespoon olive oil, plus 2 cups and more for greasing the tagine

2 cups garlic cloves, peeled (see Tip)

½ teaspoon kosher salt

1. Preheat the oven to 350°F. Grease the inside of the tagine base with olive oil.

2. Add the garlic, sprinkle it with the salt, and drizzle all over with 1 tablespoon of olive oil.

3. Transfer the uncovered tagine to the oven and roast the garlic for 20 minutes, or until it is lightly browned.

4. Let the garlic cool, transfer it to a 1-quart jar, cover with the remaining 2 cups of olive oil, seal, and store in the refrigerator for up to 2 weeks.

COOKING TIP: If you want to roast the garlic without peeling it, lightly crush the cloves with the side of a knife to smash them flat. The rest of the recipe is the same. Once they are roasted and cooled, you can discard the peels easily before storing them.

Harissa

MAKES
2½ CUPS

PREP TIME:
10 minutes

Harissa is a popular chile paste used in North African cuisine. You can buy it in most grocery stores, but this fermented fresh paste version is easy to prepare at home. The benefit of making it from scratch is you can adjust for different spice tolerances. And you can also add an assortment of herbs and spices. This recipe starts with a looser texture and less intensity, but as it ferments, a complex and rich depth of flavor develops slowly with time. It is versatile as a condiment for any food, such as tagines, marinades, sauces, grilling, and more.

5 cups chopped fresh chiles

1 whole preserved lemon, homemade (page 172) or store-bought

5 garlic cloves, peeled

1 teaspoon kosher salt

½ cup extra-virgin olive oil, plus more for topping

1. In a food processor, process the chiles, preserved lemon, garlic, and salt until blended to a smooth puree or to a slightly coarse consistency (depending on your preference).

2. Transfer the mixture to a 1-quart jar, cover the surface with olive oil, seal, and set it aside in a cool place to ferment for 2 to 3 weeks. Refrigerate the finished harissa for up to 10 months with a layer of oil on top.

VARIATION: This recipe is very simple and not as intensely spicy as you might think. I suggest you try the original first. But if that makes you nervous, you can make a milder version by adding 1 roasted sweet red bell pepper to control the heat level (and add extra flavor).

Chermoula

MAKES
1 CUP

PREP TIME:
5 minutes

Chermoula is a flavorful, tangy herb and garlic sauce that is very popular in Morocco. It pairs well with fish and seafood, which is plentiful in this country. Chermoula is traditionally used for marinades, but can be served with all kinds of meals, side dishes, dips, and sauces. This version is made with simple ingredients and the taste can be adjusted to any level of heat or acidity depending on your preference.

¼ medium preserved lemon, homemade (page 172) or store-bought

¼ cup chopped fresh cilantro

¼ cup chopped fresh parsley

2 tablespoons freshly squeezed lemon juice

4 garlic cloves, crushed and peeled

2 teaspoons kosher salt

1 teaspoon ground cumin

1 teaspoon sweet paprika

¼ teaspoon cayenne pepper, or more as desired

Extra-virgin olive oil, for topping

In a food processor, pulse the preserved lemon, cilantro, parsley, lemon juice, garlic, salt, cumin, paprika, and cayenne until blended to the desired consistency. Transfer the mixture to a jar, cover the surface with olive oil, seal, and refrigerate for up to 3 weeks.

VARIATION: You can make a red chermoula by adding 1 fresh red chile for extra heat and 1 teaspoon of tomato paste for a nice color.

Herb-Infused Olive Oil

MAKES
2 CUPS

PREP TIME:
5 minutes,
plus 1 hour
to infuse

COOK TIME:
15 minutes

This simple infused olive oil gets its flavor from aromatic fresh herbs like rosemary, oregano, thyme, basil, and others. Keep it simple and use one herb at a time, so the finished oil tastes better. You can use dried herbs if you want to keep the oil longer, because fresh herbs contain water that may encourage mold growth after several weeks of storage. Making small quantities of infused oil at a time will keep the flavor fresh once it is opened. Try it drizzled on crusty bread, hummus, feta cheese, goat cheese, or olives as a snack or appetizer.

½ cup fresh herb leaves
  (rosemary, thyme,
  oregano, dill)

2 cups extra-virgin
  olive oil

1 or 2 sprigs herb (optional)

1. Place the herbs in a small tagine and pour the olive oil over them.

2. Cover the tagine, place it on a diffuser over low heat, and cook for 10 to 15 minutes. Remove from the heat and let the mixture sit for 1 hour to infuse the oil.

3. Strain the oil into a jar (a dark color is best). If desired, add the herb sprigs to the jar (it will help identify the oil), seal, and refrigerate for up to 2 weeks.

COOKING TIP: You can also heat the oil and herbs in a heavy-bottomed saucepan over low heat.

Tagine Spice Mixes

The following spice mixes are easy to make, so it's best to make them in small batches. That way you can use them a couple times and then adjust the spices to your taste for the next batch. I did not add salt to the mixes because it must be measured separately. I highly recommend grinding some of the spices—black pepper, cumin, coriander, and cardamom—fresh every two weeks or so, because it does make a difference in taste and flavor. Try any of the different mixes in dips, soups, grains, and other non-tagine recipes for a wonderful flavor boost. And although these seasonings are labeled beef, lamb, and chicken, you will also find them in many of the seafood and vegetable recipes in this book.

Karima's Beef Spice Mix

MAKES
¼ CUP

PREP TIME:
5 minutes

1 tablespoon freshly ground black pepper

1 tablespoon ground ginger

1 tablespoon ground turmeric

1 tablespoon garlic powder

¾ teaspoon ground cardamom

In a jar, combine the pepper, ginger, turmeric, garlic powder, and cardamom. Seal and shake to combine. Store in a cool, dark place for up to 1 month.

Karima's Lamb Spice Mix

MAKES
¼ CUP

PREP TIME:
5 minutes

1 tablespoon freshly ground
   black pepper

1 tablespoon ground ginger

1 tablespoon ground turmeric

½ tablespoon ground
   cardamom

1 teaspoon ground cinnamon

⅛ teaspoon ground mace

In a jar, combine the pepper, ginger, turmeric, cardamom, cinnamon, and mace. Seal and shake to combine. Store in a cool, dark place for up to 1 month.

Karima's Chicken Spice Mix

MAKES
1 CUP

PREP TIME:
5 minutes

½ cup water

¼ medium preserved lemon,
   homemade (page 172) or
   store-bought, crushed

5 garlic cloves, minced

2 tablespoons chopped fresh
   cilantro

2 tablespoons chopped fresh
   parsley

1 teaspoon freshly ground
   black pepper

1 teaspoon ground ginger

1½ teaspoons ground turmeric

Pinch ground cinnamon

In a food processor, combine the water, preserved lemon, garlic, cilantro, parsley, pepper, ginger, turmeric, and cinnamon and puree until blended. Transfer the paste to a jar, seal, and refrigerate for up to 1 week.

MEASUREMENT CONVERSIONS

VOLUME EQUIVALENTS	U.S. STANDARD	U.S. STANDARD (OUNCES)	METRIC (APPROXIMATE)
LIQUID	2 tablespoons	1 fl. oz.	30 mL
	¼ cup	2 fl. oz.	60 mL
	½ cup	4 fl. oz.	120 mL
	1 cup	8 fl. oz.	240 mL
	1½ cups	12 fl. oz.	355 mL
	2 cups or 1 pint	16 fl. oz.	475 mL
	4 cups or 1 quart	32 fl. oz.	1 L
	1 gallon	128 fl. oz.	4 L
DRY	⅛ teaspoon	–	0.5 mL
	¼ teaspoon	–	1 mL
	½ teaspoon	–	2 mL
	¾ teaspoon	–	4 mL
	1 teaspoon	–	5 mL
	1 tablespoon	–	15 mL
	¼ cup	–	59 mL
	⅓ cup	–	79 mL
	½ cup	–	118 mL
	⅔ cup	–	156 mL
	¾ cup	–	177 mL
	1 cup	–	235 mL
	2 cups or 1 pint	–	475 mL
	3 cups	–	700 mL
	4 cups or 1 quart	–	1 L
	½ gallon	–	2 L
	1 gallon	–	4 L

OVEN TEMPERATURES

FAHRENHEIT	CELSIUS (APPROXIMATE)
250°F	120°C
300°F	150°C
325°F	165°C
350°F	180°C
375°F	190°C
400°F	200°C
425°F	220°C
450°F	230°C

WEIGHT EQUIVALENTS

U.S. STANDARD	METRIC (APPROXIMATE)
½ ounce	15 g
1 ounce	30 g
2 ounces	60 g
4 ounces	115 g
8 ounces	225 g
12 ounces	340 g
16 ounces or 1 pound	455 g

INDEX

ACKNOWLEDGMENTS

With great pleasure I would like to express my sincere thanks to Salmon Taymuree, who believed in me and my cooking skills. Also, I am so grateful to Anne Goldberg and Michelle Anderson for all the support throughout the duration of writing this cookbook. Big thanks to Leah Zarra, for her encouragement and beautiful words about this project—and I am so thankful to all who worked to develop this book behind the scenes.

My special thanks also to Sankar Raman and Roger Porter for the wonderful article about me and my passion for cooking. I would sincerely like to extend my gratitude to my kids and family, for being so kind and there for me whenever I needed them. And special thanks to my dear old friends that are close to my heart.

ABOUT THE AUTHOR

I'm Karima Elatchi. I was born and raised in Morocco—my father was from AbiJaad, and my mother was from Meknes (Amazigh)—and moved to the United States when I was thirty-six. I grew up in an extended family where the atmosphere was deeply intellectual as well as traditional. Our home was the center of my life. Being the eldest daughter, I was always next to my mom, watching and observing her cooking, but with no intention of becoming a cook, much less a chef! In fact, I graduated from the Institute of Computer Programming in Morocco, and then worked at the Treasury Department for fifteen years.

When I arrived in the United States, away from home, I realized the need to keep our family traditions alive—especially our food. I remembered the foods I loved, and that reconnection to home was vital to my joy and happiness. At the beginning of my career, I only cooked for friends and family. Soon after, I created a catering business and also shared my love of cooking by teaching workshops. As I reminisce about my life's journey, and with two grown sons of my own, I cannot help but to reflect with joy the spiritual and emotional wealth that surrounded me as I followed my dream to keep our traditional cooking alive.